KEEPING
THE DOORS OPEN

PUBLISHED BY
BRITISH AGENCIES FOR
ADOPTION & FOSTERING
11 SOUTHWARK STREET
LONDON SE1 1RQ
© BAAF 1988
ISBN 0 903534 75 4
ISSN 0260 0803
DESIGNED BY ANDREW HAIG
TYPESET BY ETHNOGRAPHICA LTD
PRINTED AND BOUND IN ENGLAND

PRACTICE SERIES: 15

Keeping the doors open

a review of post-adoption services

edited by Hedi Argent

○

BRITISH AGENCIES FOR
ADOPTION & FOSTERING

About the authors

Hedi Argent is the Post-Adoption Worker for Parents for Children
Mary Boston was Principal Child Psychotherapist at the Tavistock Clinic until she retired in 1987.
Ann Boswell is Senior Adoption Worker with the Manchester Adoption Society.
John Byng-Hall is Consultant Child Psychiatrist at the Tavistock Clinic.
Monty Cohen is Senior Social Worker with Essex County Council.
Alex Cunningham was an Adoption Specialist with Essex County Council at the time of writing.
Pauline Dancyger is a Senior Practitioner in the London Borough of Wandsworth.
Joan Fratter is a Senior Social Worker with the Barnardo's Homefinding Project in Barkingside.
Gill Gorrell-Barnes is a Senior Social Worker at the Tavistock Clinic.
Mary Griffiths-Jones is a Senior Practitioner in the London Borough of Wandsworth.
Christine Heath is a Child Psychotherapist.
Pam Hodgkins is Chairperson of NORCAP.
Margaret and Mervyn Humphreys are Social Workers with Nottinghamshire County Council. They are founders of the Triangle Group and the Child Migrant Trust.
Sandra and Douglas Hutton are adoptive parents and founder members of the Lothian Adopters Group.
Caroline Lindsey is a Consultant Child Psychiatrist at the Tavistock Clinic.
Philly Morrall is National Co-ordinator of PPIAS.
Gerry O'Hara is Regional Officer – Children and Families with the Lothian Regional Council.
Phillida Sawbridge is the Director of the Post-Adoption Centre in London.
Joan de Silva is the Post-Adoption Worker for the Independent Adoption Society.
Elisabeth Traverse is Project Leader for the Children's Society in Norwich.
Stephen Wolkind is Consultant Child Psychiatrist at the Maudsley Hospital.
Mavis Young is Principal Family Placement Officer in the City of Liverpool Social Services Department.
Other contributors (Chapter 2): *a mother whose child was adopted, a father whose child was adopted, an adoptive mother and an adopted person.*

Contents

Foreword

Doors lend a fitting image to adoption. They can be used to close in or to shut out. They can include a new child but may exclude the child's birth parents. Doors burst open when the adopted adolescent erupts, and bang to in anger when the adoptive parents can take no more. Doors which are made to swing or to revolve can make comings and goings more gentle, less sudden or less final. Some doors are made of glass: they can be seen through but they can also shatter. Some doors are solid and locked and hold secrets. Keys, to open doors, can be found or kept or lost.

A home may have many doors or it may be organised in an open plan. Parents may be heard to talk or to quarrel or to make love behind closed doors through which the adopted child may not enter. They might expect the child to knock on doors. They might also knock on the child's door before they enter.

For children who have been in care, doors are very significant. One door leads to food, another to bed. Doors which open to the child do not offer much privacy when they close, but other doors conceal mysteries. When eleven-year-old Brian showed me round his Children's Home, I pointed to a door and asked where it led. 'I don't know', he said, 'it goes nowhere, it's locked.' When Brian moved to a family, it was a long time before he could go through all the doors that were opened for him.

In 1974 Kay Donley, who was the first director of the pioneering adoption agency Spaulding for Children, in Michigan USA, came to Eastbourne, England, to open new doors for us. She told us about the older children and the children with disabilities her agency had placed. She taught us about publicity and recruitment. She urged us to prepare parents for adoption and not to vet them. And she made us believe that all kinds of people could adopt. She made us aware of the need to work directly with children and she offered us the tools to do it. Phillida Sawbridge, the first director of Parents for Children, noted everything Kay Donley said and edited it so that social workers who had not been to Eastbourne on that magical occasion might also be inspired. The book *Opening new doors* was published by ABAFA and has been reprinted by BAAF. It is still the most essential work on adoption of children with special needs, and should be used in all adoptions.

Fourteen years later, the doors Kay Donley pointed us towards have been opened, although it is still not the way everyone goes. We are placing an ever-increasing number of children with special needs, and we are preparing these children for family life. We are using plenty of publicity, and 'vetting' of adopters is giving way to 'assessment', if not always to 'preparation'. We have been building new families in a new way for some time. We know that not only must we open new doors, we have to find ways of *keeping the doors open*. Adoption goes on for ever and adoptive families have a right to a service which does not end when an adoption order is made. Nor is it enough for agencies to have an 'open door' policy. It is not only the agency's door that has to stay ajar: adoptive families need to hold their doors on the latch to allow support, when it is needed, to get in. This book is an attempt to explore how best to keep the doors open, how best to enable adoptive families, adopted children and birth parents to feel secure and undisturbed, how best to ensure that what blows in is not a sudden draught but the renewing life force of fresh air.

Hedi Argent
September 1987

Introduction

Hedi Argent

A postal survey at the end of 1985 of both local authority and voluntary adoption agencies produced an almost unanimous recognition of the need for post-adoption services and at least a wish to respond. Only one of those which replied voiced alarm about the labelling effect on adoptive families if they were to be offered special treatment, rather than be included in the usual services provided for all families. Another doubted the validity of adoption with long-term support, and would prefer families to remain foster families if this kind of support were to be required. But the agencies which expressed these concerns were those with least experience of placing children with physical, mental or severe emotional disabilities – and these same agencies are providing a counselling service for adopted people who were placed as infants, and want to trace their birth family when they are adults. This must surely be regarded not only as an essential part of adoption work but also as an integral part of any comprehensive post-adoption service.

Because the need for post-adoption work is just now coming into focus, it has been difficult to get a clear picture of what is happening here and now in various representative local authorities and voluntary agencies. We hope that this book, with contributions from statutory and voluntary agencies and from specialist groups, will at least set the scene – though the picture is changing even while this view of it is being put together. We start by describing the background, with a brief summary of the available research on the need for post-adoption support (Chapter 1). We continue with some views from consumers – an adopted person, an adoptive parent and birth parents – whose experience we need to take into account if we are to get the service right (Chapter 2). Following these are the responses from the agencies, both statutory and voluntary (Chapter 3). One long-established voluntary agency, Independent Adoption Service, has raised a grant to launch an experimental post-adoption service to replace its system of response on demand and Parents for Children, a much younger agency, which always included a post-adoption service as of right, has developed new ways of giving a regular and unrationed service to a steadily increasing number of people. More than one local authority has a tradition of post-adoption groups, as colleagues from Wandsworth write, and several voluntary agencies, like the Children's Society, Norwich, and the Manchester Adoption Society, are exploring and pioneering post-adoption work to include all adopters and adopted people within their area. Some agencies are concentrating on identifiable special needs. Transracial placements may need a very specific service; black families may wish for a service they will themselves define (Chapter 4). Other voluntary agencies and local authorities do not have precise plans for post-adoption work and most of them are limited by lack of money. They are able to maintain an informal and minimal responsive service to demands when they are made, but the costs have to be hidden because there is no existing fund to cover them. In fact two of the services described here are run by social workers in their own time on a voluntary basis, and without any statutory or formal backing.

Adoption does not concern only the child and the adoptive parents: any comprehensive service must also acknowledge the possibility of a response to the birth family. In America the 'adoption triad' is generally acknowledged and, overall, more services are available to birth parents than to adoptive parents. In this country there is one pioneering group in Nottingham, described by Margaret and Mervyn Humphries in their section on 'The Triangle group' (Chapter 5). Other local authorities and voluntary agencies offer advice and counselling to birth parents, as and when requested, but only the newly-set-up Post-Adoption Centre described by Phillida Sawbridge, and NORCAP, the National Organis-ation for Counselling Adoptees and their Parents, provide equally for everyone involved in adoption (both in Chapter 5). For, as Pam Hodgson from NORCAP explains, 'parents' means both birth and adoptive mothers and fathers.

Social occasions like annual summer picnics or Christmas parties for adoptive families have become an accepted and affectionate part of post-adoption support, especially in the voluntary sector. It is where families meet and encourage each other. It is where growth and progress are monitored and most appreciated. After all, only another adoptive parent will know how it feels when a damaged and damaging adolescent gives a Christmas card which says 'Thank you for being a good Mum and Dad'. Social occasions can even extend to residential weekends with workshops, as offered by at least one agency (Christian

10

Outreach) to families who have adopted from overseas – an example of post-adoption service aimed at a group about whom relatively little is known as yet. But most significant of all is the movement of adoptive families to form their own support groups. Parent-to-Parent Information on Adoption Services (PPIAS) organises its own events, publishes a journal with photolists of children who need families and offers a mutual counselling service as well as expert advice and information (Chapter 5).

Children who are 'hard to place' are not going to be easy to bring up, but even ordinary, healthy infants and their adoptive parents may at some time experience problems with that extra family ingredient, 'adoption'. Dr Stephen Wolkind from the Maudsley Hospital, Dr John Byng-Hall, Mary Boston and colleagues from the Tavistock Centre, and Claudia Jewett from Boston all have a special interest in adoption and all of them see children in their clinics who were 'hard to place' but they also see baby adoption families. Their contributions to this book (Chapter 6) reflect different therapeutic techniques and perspectives and they do not always agree, but they all recognise the need to acknowledge the adoption factor, and they all respond by offering an informed and alert post-adoption service.

For many of us, it all started in America, and we bring this book to an end by looking at what is happening there now (Chapter 7) and by considering, in Chapter 8, the way ahead.

1 Why a post-adoption service?

Gerry O'Hara

The research background

The last few years have seen a change in the circumstances of the children being referred for adoption. Those identified by Rowe and Lambert[1] in 1973 are now largely grown up and by the early 1980s the backlog of such children had been cleared. It is our experience and has been suggested (Triseliotis)[2] that those children had been in institutions over lengthy periods of time and members of their original families had either disappeared or had totally lost interest in them. Triseliotis goes on to point out that many of the children needing new families now '(1) have come into care when older; (2) have been in care for a shorter period of time, and (3) are far more likely not only to be in touch with a member of the original family but also to have a meaningful attachment to such a person or people'. The experience of both the families who adopted the 'children who wait' and more recent adopters challenges us to develop a continuing support service to cover all adoptions as well as meeting the new demands of current placements of children with emotional, physical and mental disabilities.

A recent review of children identified for adoption in Lothian reveals that children have typically had several periods in care, usually between two and four years continuously before they are placed. In some cases planning for adoption has happened at a much earlier stage but legal delays have contributed to children waiting in temporary care. The children placed are invariably seen by our adoptive parents as problematic, although the symptoms shown by the children – who have usually experienced separation and loss at a very early stage – vary. Usually a feeling that the child has not really attached to the new parents is borne out by a range of different behavioural problems which can be seen as manifestations of poor early and subsequent attachments. Lying and stealing are most common. Children who have been adopted at school age are likely to under-achieve at school, frequently have problems in making and sustaining peer relationships and can be seen as not trusting their adoptive parents. Often these behavioural problems are still present several years after the granting of an adoption order. This 'practice wisdom' view has been borne out by a small study of ten adoptive families of 'special-needs' children involved with Lothian's homefinding team.[3]

Some adoption workers have repeatedly pointed out the need for ongoing support. Spaulding for Children[4] expected that families would have difficulties in bringing up their adopted children throughout their childhood and possibly into adult life. They considered post-adoption support of their placements and the partnership between social worker and family to be vital. Jewett[5] emphasised that it was normal for adopters to have doubts, feelings of hopelessness and depression on some occasions, particularly as they realised that some of the problems were intractable. She considered there was a strong need for support to be readily available by the adoption agency. Donley[6] saw 'survivability' as the primary consideration of the placement and her view was that 'placement workers must believe that strong supportive services are normal and act accordingly'.

Voluntary agencies in this country concentrating on the placement of special-needs children have stated their commitment to post-placement support and have described their work. Sawbridge[7] said that the plan for the Parents for Children adoption agency was to offer an open-ended time commitment to every family with whom they placed a child. A team approach to support was developed to ensure the availability of agency staff. Argent[8] suggested that by staying in touch with Parents for Children families were able to make contact in a crisis and to be sure of a helpful response. She considered that there were three main tasks in post-placement work: to enable families to 'claim' the child as their own; to act as a mirror and a sounding board to help families measure their own progress and to put families in touch with relevant groups, agencies or specialists. Macaskill,[9, 10] found that for adoptive families, informal networks were not sufficient support. The specialist skills of the placing agency were felt by the families to be most necessary when crises occurred. Yates[11] similarly found that the support of the specialist homefinders and the understanding of fellow adopters was important. The majority of Lothian families in her study felt that their informal networks were not always sufficient and that there was a need for specialist skills. She found that many adopters preferred 'to discuss the day-to-day problems of their child with their homefinder rather than with their family or friends'. Some adopters felt disloyal to the child if they talked to family and friends about the problems or the feelings that the children sometimes engendered in them: 'You want the family to accept your child and not to be put off. I don't tell them the problems.' Adopters commonly felt that people with children of their own failed to allow for the difficult background experiences the adopted child had gone through and tended either to offer inappropriately punitive advice or to dismiss the problems:

'Neighbours – don't bank on them when it comes to the crunch.'

'Friends, I discovered, turned out to be no support: they made me feel inferior because she was not born to me.'

'I learned to keep my mouth shut – you find out who your friends are.'

Overall, Yates[12] found that whilst the support of family and friends was important, the understanding of other adopters and the support of the homefinding agency were of crucial help.

Adopters' views

The recent Adoption Agencies Regulations include provisions for 'advice and assistance to the prospective adopters'. Thoburn et al,[13] evaluating the Children's Society project 'The child wants a home', concluded that the style which found most favour with parents and children had as major ingredients consultation, quality control and, when necessary, co-therapy with the new parents.

Yates[14] found the following to be important:
– interest and commitment to the new family
– warmth and the ability to listen
– problem-sharing without reservation – meaning both tension release and problem solving (adopters' perceptions)
– someone able to 'stand back'
– reinforcement of adopters' parental authority
– competence over official matters, the sharing of information about the child, reliability, trustworthiness and availability.

Interestingly, the child's own social worker was often seen as unhelpful. Complaints about their description of the child and their perception of the child's problems were common and the worker's link with the child's past was resented by some adopters. In general, even when the child was close to the social worker, most adopters preferred the child's social worker to be involved for as short a time as possible and in some cases, where involvement continued, this had not helped the relationship.

Summary

Families seem to appreciate the need and value of post-placement support from their own adoption worker (as distinct from the child's social worker) and seem able broadly to define what they find helpful. Families also seem to experience their own support networks (i.e. friends, families and neighbours) as less helpful than they had expected before placement, but the support of other adopters, and the understanding they bring, seems to be important.

The need for post-placement and post-adoption support has been strongly evidenced from the experience of placement workers and increasingly from various studies of adoptive families. Social workers can no longer see adoption as a solution in itself for the problems of children who have experienced great trauma in early childhood. We are now acknowledging the sometimes irrevocable damage which has been done to such children and we must face up to the consequences: that is, support for the families who give so much to them.

References

1 Rowe J and Lambert L *Children who wait* ABAFA, 1973.

2 Triseliotis J *Adoption & Fostering* 9 4 1985.

3 Yates P 'Post-placement support for adoptive families of hard-to-place children' MSc Research study, Edinburgh University, 1985.

4 Unger C, Dwashino G and Johnson E *Chaos, madness and unpredictability* Spaulding for Children, 1977.

5 Jewett C L *Adopting the older child* Harvard Common Press, 1978.

6 Donley K S 'Beyond placement': Paper presented at BAAF conference 'Making and sustaining placements', 1984.

7 Sawbridge P (1980) 'Seeking new parents: a decade of development' in Triseliotis J (ed) *New developments in foster care and adoption* Routledge and Kegan Paul, 1980.

8 Argent H 'I have a family now' in Sawbridge P (ed) *Parents for children* BAAF, 1983.

9 Macaskill C 'Post-adoption support: is it essential?' *Adoption & Fostering* 9, 1 1985.

10 Macaskill C 'Who should support after adoption?' *Adoption & Fostering* 9, 2 1985.

11 See 3 above.

12 See 3 above

13 Thoburn J, Murdoch A and O'Brien A 'Routes to permanence: CWAH Evaluation' *Adoption & Fostering* 9, 1 1985.

14 See 3 above.

2 The need – from the consumer viewpoint

The consumers of any post-adoption service on offer include not only adoptive parents and their children but also birth parents and adults adopted as children. In this chapter we include the experience of a birth mother and a birth father, both of whom feel that they would have benefited from post-adoption support, as well as that of an adoptive parent who received inept and inadequate support and an adopted person.

A birth mother

I became pregnant in 1964 when I was 16. My parents were very shocked and upset, but supported me in the way they thought best – by deciding that I should have the baby adopted. My two sisters, aged 14 and 15, were not told that I was pregnant and in the five months I stayed at home I did not discuss my feelings with anyone. Only once do I remember my mother referring to it, when she asked me whether I had felt any sign of movement. I said no, which was a lie.

When I was about four months pregnant my mother drove me to another town to meet a social worker. I don't remember her speaking to me – I don't think she did. I sat on her elegant settee feeling very ashamed, while she and my mother made arrangements for me to go into a mother and baby home. I did not see or hear from her again.

Four weeks before my baby was expected, my mother and aunt took me to the home. I stayed there until I had to go into hospital for the birth, which took place at 4.15 in the morning. It was a forceps delivery after a very long, lonely, and painful labour. I named the baby Paul.

It was compulsory at that hospital to breast-feed. I had not been told in advance and it was a bit of a shock. Now I am so pleased I was able to have done this for him.

I loved my time in hospital. My father visited me quite often as he went to sea and his boat docked nearby. I found out later that he went to a great deal of trouble to do this. He died four years ago and we never talked about my baby.

I remember in hospital when I saw all the fathers coming in to see their babies, I felt very strongly that I had no right to have given birth to this baby in these circumstances. I felt it was a terrible sin to have a baby without a father or anything to offer it. I felt so sorry for my son because he was at a disadvantage. I knew, in hospital, that adoption would be best for him.

We moved back to the home. I did not have a photo of my baby. I remember one of the other girls smuggled a camera in and took one secretly of hers. I was shocked at her breaking the rules. Over the years I have longed for a photograph. It would have meant so much. One day, he looked at me and smiled properly. I was standing by his cot and intense happiness turned to intense grief. I did not cry but felt paralysed and physically incapable of walking away. The next day he was taken by his new parents. I was told a little about them, but not allowed to meet them. I tried to look out of the window when they were due, but I was afraid of breaking the rules so I missed them. I was absolutely devastated and distraught when I saw the empty cot.

My mother came to fetch me home. We did not mention the baby during the journey home. My sisters returned from school and we behaved as if nothing had happened. Later, I had to sign the final adoption papers. I really did think it was best for him, but I also knew at this stage it was not the best for *me*.

Whenever anything to do with adoption came up in the following years, I often felt deeply hurt by people's comments and felt isolated. I did not discuss my past with anyone and for years I suffered in silence. Until I joined Triangle (see Chapter 5), my husband was the only person who understood and shared in some way my feelings of loss, which have sometimes been very acute. At those times I need to talk, to grieve and in a way live through the experiences again. Although I have four children I am always aware that I really have five. He will always be the first and I am very aware that he is now an adult. When he turned 18, I hoped he would try to find me. Indeed, by the time he was 19 I became aware that I would hate to end my life without him ever wanting to find out about me. I also became concerned that he may not even know he has been adopted. I now feel very strongly that everyone should know if they are adopted.

There must be many people like me who had children adopted 20 to 30 years ago. Some will be waiting, in hope or dread, to be traced by the child they gave for adoption. There is a desperate need for a professional service to be available to prepare and support them – just to talk to people who understand, at the times in their life when they feel the need, is so vital.

A birth father
As an only child with a protected childhood, I was an immature 24. At a group summer holiday I had a relationship not even deserving the description of 'holiday romance'. The last evening's alcoholic intake, the late night walk along the beach, the fumbling intimacies: the following morning, slightly embarrassed and relieved goodbyes. Two months elapsed and then came the shattering news of a pregnancy. Brief options about marriage were considered and quickly abandoned in spite of current attitudes to illegitimacy. The mother's family took the decision on adoption to which I readily agreed and I footed the bills. The event was clouded in secrecy on all sides, for which I was grateful. I was even able to keep the event entirely hidden from my family and friends at home. At the time it seemed an incredible 'let off': it was unbelievable that I could 'get away with it'.

When the day arrived, twins were born and after one brief glimpse I was excluded with the, as I then thought, understandable instruction to make no further contact. I was free to wipe out the whole episode and get on with my life! Could this be true? Could I get away with this for a few hundred pounds? How quickly that relief passed and was displaced by occasional totally unexpected flashes from the sub-conscious – a mixture of guilt, curiosity, the certainty of something missing, sublimated in the pace of life and a career and other relationships including, eventually, marriage.

How good it could have been with a clear conscience as a foundation for a total commitment – if only. Inevitably the guilty secret asserted itself. Having been told by my doctor, whom I had consulted in desperation, to 'forget about it and get on with your life', I found the dishonesty of my position to be a totally destructive element in the marriage. Life was almost like running a marathon with a stone in one's shoe – absolutely crippling emotionally. The guilt increased with every commitment of the girl I had married who, knowing something was wrong, tried endlessly throughout 23 years of our marriage to sort out our relationship. Despite some good times, and two fantastic children – only aware of occasional rows and guilt-provoked scenes between their parents – the inevitable break-up resulted. Had it not been for a

19

conversation with a friend from the Triangle Group (see Chapter 5), I would still be hiding my guilt and confusion.

Unfortunately the revelation to my wife came too late to save our relationship and the break-up of my beloved family, but the strength which the group gave me to make that confession at least enabled her and my children to understand so much. If only I had received such help sooner! A birth father is still a human being and it is crucial that the deep emotional problems caused and suffered by such an experience as I had can be mitigated, in the future, by the development of professional, post-adoption services.

An adoptive parent

I have five children: two daughters born to me, aged 18 and six, plus three adopted children – Mike, an Irish/West Indian child who came to me aged eleven months; Jonathan, who came at 18 months, labelled as having Down's syndrome; and Bridget, who came last, aged eleven and a half, following the breakdown of her previous placement.

I have longed for real post-adoption support frequently in the past few years. I've had to deal with the problems faced by Jonathan, who does not have Down's syndrome after all but is handicapped in some way which causes him to have difficulty communicating and to be below average development; by Bridget, who found adjustment to family life extremely hard having had a history of breakdowns and being, in addition, a black child in a white family; and by Mike – again, a black child in a white family working through his identity confusion.

Worst of all, I think, was my ignorance of the causes behind the behaviour problems and the frustrations involved in trying to get outside help. Even when we found our way to the child guidance clinic we felt we didn't fit the usual criteria so it proved difficult to use what was offered. For example, by the time Jonathan was three years old we were certain his development was well below normal and he was referred for psychological assessment. When we were seen by the consultant and staff we felt they were distracted by that fact that we were not his birth parents, their opinion being that we were making unfair comparisons with the two bright children born to us. We were unable to convince them of our ability to judge Jonathan's behaviour and they told us he was within the 'broad bands of normality'.

At the same time I joined a group for mothers of children with disabilities run by a social worker who told me later that they were in the rather odd position of having to treat me like a 'fellow professional' as I was not Jonathan's natural mother. I felt I had the worst of all worlds! As a mother I felt I should be able to question and understand the treatment of my child. On the other hand I couldn't identify with most of the discussions about birth and guilt feelings about having a handicapped child which didn't apply to me. Far from feeling guilty, we loved Jonathan and felt it must be possible to make life a bit more comprehensible for him.

We were encouraged in a well-meaning and totally frustrating way to keep on providing a happy environment for Jonathan. We felt we didn't know how to keep him happy because we didn't understand the nature of slow development and we wanted information about children with communication problems. We were unsure of how to proceed with him and felt defeated – that we had failed him. By the time Jonathan was ten and a half we had him assessed again and were told he needed not less than three sessions of psychotherapy per week for some years. It was heartbreaking to be proved right after years of feeling that he should be getting help.

Next time at the child guidance clinic I was told that it was usual for the mother to see the social worker once a week to iron out any problems that might arise as a result of the therapy being done with Jonathan. I was relieved to find a supportive set-up because I had no experience of psychotherapy, no concept of length of treatment, side effects for the rest of the family or even what its potential was. However, at our first session the social worker said she knew nothing about the therapist's methods with Jonathan and she couldn't advise me about his behaviour because as I had managed him so long I was really the expert. After all she had never even met Jonathan! I spent a lot of time assuring her of my commitment to Jonathan's course of therapy in spite of the fact that he had already lived with us for nine years and we had put much care and effort into his upbringing. I felt our discussions were designed for a natural mother and were based on exploring guilt feelings. Perhaps the social worker was uncomfortable in this situation too, because I attended the clinic for a year and in all that time she never actually called me by my name. In no way was it a supportive experience.

In our experience of adoption, open discussion and sharing of information before placement was the norm: how disconcerting it was to meet professionals afterwards who were threatened by our expectations. We badly needed a safe environment in which to question the suitability of help being offered for Jonathan.

When Bridget came to live with us she had already experienced separation and disaster. Her social worker said she was emotionally disturbed and unable to make relationships. We had no experience to put real meaning to those words because we knew no other parents who had successfully worked through that situation. Bridget felt she had tried hard in the previous placement and it had still broken down, so she had nothing to encourage her to believe that effort was worthwhile. We were all aware that another family had been unable to cope with her, so from time to time we were overwhelmed by our difficulties and gave up on each other.

Bridget had a very poor self-image and was confused about her sexual identity. She cultivated male mannerisms, dressed like a boy and aggressively asserted that she was a boy – even changing her name to Brian. We had no idea how to tackle this delicate situation and felt we shouldn't do anything about her behaviour until we understood what it meant. At the child guidance clinic a very feminine psychologist told us that she herself often wore jeans – that was how the modern liberated girl dressed! I didn't think she was taking us very seriously and again our ability to judge abnormal behaviour in a child not born to us was in doubt. I knew my friends' teenage girls were not behaving like Bridget – but then they had not been through her upheavals. We went home feeling we had failed again and very aware of how we could do this damaged child more harm. Her behaviour upset the other children, especially as she seemed hell-bent on destroying the whole family. Though we tried to reassure them, they sensed our confusion too. At the time they could have done with some special support for themselves. Also, it was very hard for relatives and grandparents to stand by and see emotional upheaval caused to their grandchildren by another child brought into the family. They felt that it affected their relationship with the children. Perhaps relatives need someone to talk through their feelings with them too, when parents are involved in more immediate problems.

Though we had tried to prepare our children for when Bridget came, we had not really been able to anticipate what their problems might be. Mike was eight when she joined us, and he refused to recognise her as a member of his family in school. Because they're both black he felt his friends would think she was his natural sister and her odd behaviour embarrassed him. It would have been marvellous at that time to tap into other families' experiences to see how their children coped with comments from friends and teachers. Our social worker had tried to prepare us but we just hadn't the experience to understand words like emotional deprivation and poor relationships. We had never seen what those phrases meant in day-to-day living in a family.

With Mike we had had really constructive help when he was three years old and still very unsettled. We found a social worker who realised that adoption did not automatically solve the problems of hyperactive, institutionalised children. She explained with great kindness how he might be feeling and why, and helped us to sort out our real feelings and worries about him.

Then when Mike was fourteen he began to explore what it meant to him to be black. He joined black youth groups and explored black culture. We felt totally excluded because we knew no one in the new groups and felt we would be unable to reach him to offer help if he got into any kind of difficulties. We had always had a very happy relationship with Mike and we knew he was doing his best not to hurt us. He was confused as to how to confirm his membership of a black group and yet risk meeting his white parents on the street. It was a frightening time for us. We were making up the rules as we went along without any experience to call upon and did not know where to turn for advice.

So we were a family that needed lots of help in the years after our children came to us. Most parents have problems but they can help to sort out their attitudes and feelings by talking to friends with similar experiences. Of course this applies to adoptive parents too, only some of our children have more complicated problems and so we need more experience and expertise to be available to us.

An adopted person
People function on many different levels: what is of help to one person may seem like an intrusion to another. So the compulsory counselling enforced by the 1975 Children Act for people adopted before 1976 can prove either a beneficial experience for the adopted person or an invasion of privacy – indeed, to some people the phrase 'compulsory counselling' seems like a contradiction in terms. The benefits gained largely depend on the counsellor. He or she may be a competent interviewer, able to collate information and put it to good use, but

without a non-judgemental approach – a 'listening ear' – and some empathy with the adopted person, the effects of the counselling are likely to be negative rather than helpful. In my own experience, counselling amounted to a conversation dotted with comments like 'why bother?' and 'you won't find anything'. It seems likely, therefore, that those with personal experience both of the emotional turmoil involved and of the desire to become aware of one's family background will be the most effective counsellors.

If the adopted person decides to approach their birth relatives, they need to feel in control of the search – as well as being aware of the implications. At some points in the process, the feelings of isolation and desperation can become unbearable. For me, the help of a network of people with personal experience of the triangle (both birth and adoptive parents as well as adopted people) was invaluable. Knowing that someone was at the end of the phone, someone who understood and would give me time, was so important. A self-help group like NORCAP can have much more to offer than an 'objective' counsellor. On the other hand, of course, some people prefer to carry out their search alone, and their feelings too must be respected. They may consider group meetings and telephone conversations not only unnecessary but intrusive, and will certainly resist any attempt by the counsellor to 'take over'. Their need can best be met by supplying practical details of how to search along with lists of organisations that can help.

It seems that all those involved in the adoption triangle have at some point suffered from the effects of guilt: an emotion often encouraged by the negative and ill-informed views of family, community or society at large. The birth mother may feel guilty for having conceived a child she could not bring up, having concealed the problems from family and colleagues, having wondered whether or not to keep the child and, having decided on adoption, having to endure the grief at parting and often the following years of regret. Adoptive parents may feel that the only way of coping with the child who asks difficult and direct questions is to build a fantasy world to gloss over the reality. In later years when the truth comes out – as it invariably does – they may excuse their guilt by saying that 'we shouldn't really have wanted to know'. Finally there is the guilt carried by the adopted person – 'What did I do wrong?', 'Why didn't they want me?' – making that anxiety the cause of anything that goes wrong. All this is futile. We must stop apportioning blame; one side of the triangle is not superior to any other. We must be truthful and honest, talk openly with those who need to know, leave fantasy to the brothers Grimm.

3 The response – from the agencies

The following are accounts of a range of post-adoption services offered by voluntary and statutory agencies. These are not the only services in existence nor does the range necessarily cover every aspect of a comprehensive post-adoption service. But these responses give a fair indication of what is possible and available and what is to be hoped for in the future.

MANCHESTER ADOPTION SOCIETY
Ann Boswell

Support groups

Post-adoption support has been an accepted part of our agency service for several years. In September 1978, an adoption worker and a manager/adoption panel member attended a five-day residential course in Sheffield organised by BAAF and led by Kay Donley. One of our tasks was to plan a new piece of work for the agency and to report back at a day seminar the following February (which concentrated the mind wonderfully). We had already begun to tackle the challenging work of finding families for children and family groups past the baby stage and post-adoption support was an obvious area for development. All our placements are now 'special needs' children.

By February 1979 we had written to all our families in order to assess the level of need and, by the end of the year, three geographically-based groups had been set up. Two of the groups have since been amalgamated and we now have a North Manchester and a South Manchester group. Each group includes two adoption workers and two adoption panel members and meets every six to eight weeks. Each has developed its own style, largely generated by the members who decide what the agenda of each meeting should be. Some sessions are about a specific topic such as 'education', 'adolescence' or 'telling', and may involve an outside speaker with a special interest in, and understanding of, adoption. Others are more informal and provide the opportunity for parents to exchange ideas and information and to discuss specific problems. The meetings take place in the evening but once a year there is a picnic or an afternoon party to which all the children are invited with their parents. Everyone brings food and games to share and the children enjoy being at a function where adoption is 'the norm'.

New applicants are encouraged to join the support groups as soon as they fill in an application form, because they learn so much more from other adopters than we could ever convey as mere adoption workers. The principle of partnership is thus firmly established from the beginning and the need for support is seen as a natural part of adoption, and not as an admission of failure. New adopters are impressed by the honesty between workers and families and reassured to find that there is no such thing as 'the perfect parent' (or the perfect worker, for that matter!).

Discussion tends to take the heat out of a situation and get things in proportion. It is interesting to hear most of the couples say that they thought they had problems until they hear what the others had to put up with! Sharing difficulties with other parents can often prevent a situation deteriorating into the familiar 'downward spiral' of tension, bad behaviour and recrimination. Many adopters say that they need to talk to people who understand the added dimension of adoption and the effect that separation and several moves can have upon children, many years after joining their permanent family.

Meetings are relaxed, open, informative, funny and, occasionally, bawdy. We, as workers, learn a tremendous amount from listening to adopters who are several years on from placement and we are cheered by the determination, humour and sense of achievement which is constantly demonstrated. The other side of this coin, however, is when really serious problems arise which, with hindsight, could have been anticipated. This is the most effective learning experience of all and a cogent argument for working with adoptive families long enough for this to happen.

Transracial placements

The current debate about same-race placements has led to an increasing awareness within the agency for the importance for black children of being brought up in a family of similar racial and cultural origins. We have become increasingly troubled about the transracial placements we made in the past and conscious of the possibly unmet needs of both children and adoptive parents in these families. We considered that not only should we be more positive about recruiting black families, but we should also support the transracial placements we had already made in as constructive a way as possible. In 1984 we wrote to all our families who had adopted a black child and subsequently held two meetings, the first of which was addressed by a black social worker who is also an adoptive mother. The group has been meeting ever since and black social workers and adopters have helped us in all the sessions. Many controversial issues have been discussed and members of the group have been very honest about their views and feelings. It has been a thought-provoking and, at times, painful experience for all of us, but we have learnt a great deal. We have discussed practical ways of helping and equipping children to cope with racism and to grow up with a positive sense of their own black identity. It is important that heightened awareness leads to positive action and does not stop short at the discussion stage.

Individual support
Apart from the groups, we are always available to see people on an individual basis. Birth parents sometimes keep in touch for many years, asking for news of their child through the agency and keeping us informed of their own circumstances. One mother, who is gay, asked for her seven-year-old daughter to be placed for adoption eleven years ago and still calls in occasionally. She loved her child but wanted her to have a more traditional family than she could provide. She is reassured to know that at 18 her daughter is happy in her family and has an interesting job. Adopted children placed through this agency as babies during the last 21 years are now coming back for more information about their origins. It is a fascinating task to look through the old records on microfilm and to build up a pen picture of the background information. Sadly, some of the earlier records are very sparse and highlight the need to collect information meticulously at the time of placement.

Adoptive parents may need individual help with problems which are too complex or too personal to discuss in the group. This can often be provided by the adoption worker, in family sessions or in individual work with children. Sometimes, the placement of a second child reactivates feelings and memories for the first child who may need to 'rework' the past or even look at it properly for the first time. One little girl of nine (placed at four years) exhibited some extremely obnoxious behaviour when a little boy of two joined the family. The adoption worker helped the parents tackle control issues and did some joint work with them and the child, going over her past and collecting more photographs of significant people and places. Relationships within the family are much improved and the child has gained in security and confidence.

Some families benefit from referral to other professionals, such as child psychiatrists, educational psychologists, paediatricians etc, and a network of links with specialists who understand adoption is an important part of our post-adoption service. We try not to overburden sympathetic colleagues in other professions, but we find their input invaluable.

Non-agency work

An increasing proportion of our post-adoption work is with people who are not directly involved with our agency but who need specialist advice about adoption. They write or telephone because we are listed under 'Adoption' in the telephone directory. Most of the calls are from adopted people or birth parents who are unable to contact their original agency. Response varies according to need. Some only require a leaflet or a referral to another agency. Others require more time-consuming help. One birth mother phoned recently because the daughter she had placed for adoption sixteen years before had contacted her. The daughter's boyfriend had called out of the blue, having made his own investigations. The mother felt strongly that her daughter should tell her adoptive parents before she would agree to a meeting. She asked for our help and, eventually, we were able to work with her, the adopters and the girl, towards a meeting which was a positive experience for everyone.

We feel that this service should be available to any member of the 'adoption triangle' and that it should be staffed by workers who are experienced in the field of adoption and child care and who understand the delicate issues involved. We see it as part of the comprehensive adoption service which should be provided by every local authority and adoption agency, whether they do the work themselves or contract it out.

29

In conclusion

We feel that post-adoption support is a vital part of adoption work as a whole, and that adopters, children and natural parents should be able to use it as of right. As workers, we cannot hope to improve our practice in the future if we do not learn from the placements we have made in the past. It is not always a comfortable process – talk about 'keeping the doors open', we feel like slamming them at times! – but our responsibility doesn't end just because the adoption order is made. Our most valuable resource is undoubtedly the pool of experienced adopters already known to the agency but we, as workers, need to be imaginative and available, particularly in times of stress.

LIVERPOOL SOCIAL SERVICES
Mavis Young

'The need to know': adoption counselling under section 26 of the Children Act 1975

'The adoption order is granted' and the social worker leaves court, goes back to the office and closes the file with a feeling of satisfaction. Perhaps the most important lesson that has been learnt from counselling adult adopted people is that the file may not be closed for ever. It may well be opened up again 18, 30 or even 60 years later. The adoption process is a continuing one. The *legal* ties between the child and birth parents are permanently severed by the making of the adoption order but the need to know about one's origins, which is for most people a natural curiosity, can for some adopted people become essential in working out their own identity. All social workers involved in counselling have heard comments like 'I want to find out who I really am', 'I want to fill in the gaps in my life', 'I just want to see my mother'. These people speak of the need to know about themselves, what their birth parents were like and why they were placed for adoption.

Section 26 of the Children Act 1975, which was implemented on 26 November 1976, enables adopted adults over the age of 18 years and resident in Great Britain to apply to the Registrar General for access to their original birth record (following the Scottish example). The adopted person seeking this information is required to apply to the Registrar General in Titchfield, Hampshire, giving brief details of their adopted name, age and date of adoption, if known. The Registrar will then refer them to a 'counsellor', as anyone adopted before 12 November 1976 must have a meeting with a counsellor before being given the personal details which would enable them to obtain a copy of their birth certificate. Those adopted since 12 November 1976 may see a counsellor if they wish but are not obliged to do so. Counselling services are available at the General Register Office in London and must be offered by the local authority where the applicant is resident or the local authority where the court made the adoption order. This chapter is based on the experience of counselling in one local authority social services department.

Counselling in Liverpool Social Services is undertaken by five of the family placement officers, two of the five involved bearing the main burden of responsibility; in all cases counselling is in addition to their other duties as family placement officers. It was felt that counselling should be undertaken by social workers who have had experience of the whole process of adoption and after ten years of implementation of the Act this view is still held. The experience of working with birth parents and adoptive parents, a knowledge of the law and a historical perspective of adoption policy helps the social worker to tell the adopted person about their adoption and how their birth parents and adoptive parents may have felt. There are also vital lessons for the social workers to be learned through meeting adults adopted as children, which should have some impact on their current adoption practice. Counsellors must be aware, for example, of how important the initial interview is to the applicant and should arrange an appointment without delay, ensuring that they are there to meet the applicant on time, whatever other crises may be going on in the office.

In the last ten years 229 adopted people have been referred to the department by the Registrar General and 574 other enquiries have been made. These are mostly from adopted people or from other social workers seeking information from the records of a large local voluntary adoption agency which is no longer in operation but has placed its records, numbering 5,300, in the department for safe keeping. We also hold the records of placements made by our own agency since 1948. Finding the files – which are kept in a dark, musty cellar in a separate building – and recording enquiries create pressures, as no additional clerical help has been provided. The whole issue of making appropriate records and preserving them is one that needs careful attention from social workers and administrative staff. Counselling has shown how important simple basic information about the birth parents, their background, physical characteristics, racial identity, hobbies and interests can be to the adopted person, and how disappointing it is when all the record says is: 'The mother is a single woman'.

For the counsellors the experience of meeting adopted adults is always stimulating, sometimes enjoyable and sometimes stressful depending on the needs of the applicant – what they are seeking and how far they can be helped. The legislation requires that there should be an interview but many applicants return for more help and discussion and some keep in touch for years.

The experience in Liverpool Social Services about who applies for information and what they are seeking corresponds very closely to the results of a survey which was carried out by Alfred Leeding in the West Midlands Area and a study by Cyril Day of the first 500 interviews at the General Register Office in London. (Both of these research projects were written up in the booklet *Access to birth records* published by BAAF in 1980.)

Slightly more women than men apply. Ages range from 18 to 66 but most are in the 25 to 35 years age group. Many were adopted in the war years, mostly as babies up to one year of age. The majority speak of a good satisfactory relationship with their adoptive parents although a few reported unhappy relationships and two had been removed from their placement following ill-treatment or neglect. Very few applicants know much about their adoption or how they came to be adopted and very rarely are the adoptive parents aware that they are making enquiries about their origins. In only two cases have the adoptive parents come with the adopted person to the interview. In most cases, therefore, there has been very little open communication about adoption. Some had been 'told' they were adopted but very little else. Some found out much later in an argument or from other people and in three cases it was not until after the death of the adoptive parent that the truth was known. It is not surprising, therefore, that the majority of these adopted people are seeking information about themselves: obtaining a birth certificate was one step in this process.

In our experience very few adopted people are content with the birth information alone: most want to know more and seek information from the court record or adoption agency record, and a few have gone on to trace their birth parents with varying degrees of success, and faced pleasure or disappointment at the outcome. Sometimes tracing the birth parents is the only way that answers to some of the adopted person's questions can be found. It is usually the birth mother, but in some cases the birth father, they wish to know about – to know why they were placed for adoption and what has happened to the parents since their birth.

Maureen came to the department to be counselled the day after the Act was implemented. She was then 40 and desperately wanted to find her birth mother. She eventually traced her to the USA and has been to see her on several occasions and she has met her half-sister and quite a large extended family. She is still in touch with the counsellor ten years later as she now wants to find her father. But she also admits to some misgivings about having found her birth family, as they are involving her in family feuds and squabbles with which she cannot cope.

Daniel, aged 18, wanted to meet his mother and was very disappointed when he did as she wasn't at all like he had though she might be. Although he was disappointed, now that he is older and more mature he looks back on the meeting with gratitude and sees that it helped him to sort himself out. His adoptive parents supported him throughout the search.

Enid wanted to find her mother. She was traced but resisted meeting Enid. She continually posponed the meeting she had initially agreed to. This was extremely distressing for Enid who could only see this as another rejection.

Elaine wanted to meet her mother but her mother was reluctant, feeling that Elaine would blame her for placing her for adoption. They did meet and felt comfortable with each other. They looked very alike. They were pleased that they could support and help each other.

Counsellors have become aware that the interview for the adopted person is a personal and important meeting. Even the most self-assured applicant can find the receipt of such personal information as their original name and place of birth quite unnerving. Although they may retain an apparent composure they often come back later for more discussion and say that they have not been able to sleep. The need to know 'who I am' may have become even more pressing because the adopted person comes to the first interview with one identity and goes out with two. Most adopted people seem to value the opportunity of talking to someone who is knowledgeable but not emotionally involved in their adoption experience and most accept the need to think through what it could mean for them and for anyone else who may be affected, if they wish to trace their birth parents.

Counsellors can face dilemmas about their role. A research study on the working of Section 26 of the Children Act completed by Erica Haimes and Noel Timms for the DHSS describes the different strategies that counsellors may use (*Adoption, identity and social policy* Gower 1985). They typified them as the 'enablers', the 'detectives' and the 'safeguarders'. The 'enablers' will make themselves available to the adopted person for contact and discussion, will help to obtain records and share the information in the records and act as an intermediary if they wish to contact the birth family. But they will not do all the leg-work of searching through registers or visiting old neighbours. The 'detectives' will do this, as they probably like finding and following clues! The 'safeguarders' will be those counsellors who are so concerned by the adopted person's attitude or immaturity or even mental ill health that they will not want to give more than the basic details that they are required to give. Counsellors probably employ all these strategies at different times according to the needs of the individual applicant but, in Liverpool, the counsellors have seen themselves mainly in the enabling role, feeling that adopted people have the right to adoption information and to trace their origins. There can be real ethical dilemmas about this. Promises to birth parents may have to be broken to meet the needs of the adopted person. The request for help may come from a natural sibling seeking an adopted sibling. The legislation does not suggest that the initiative can work in this direction, but it is within the discretion of the counsellors to help. How protective should we be when adults with a need to know are involved?

There are stresses in the work. Adopted people may be very anxious to trace their birth parents – becoming, sometimes, obsessed with their quest. If the birth parent can be traced, the contact will inevitably come as a shock and they will have to be 'counselled' as well! They may be angry and apprehensive because their family is unaware, they may be anxious or delighted or just need time to adjust to the idea, but the counsellor can be put under pressure from two directions: birth parent and adopted person. Meetings between the parties, whether joyful or disappointing, are always nerve-racking. Afterwards, the counsellor's role could be short-lived. The adopted person, birth family and adoptive family may go on to work out for themselves how to adjust to this new situation and sometimes to new relationships. A few of those involved will need help and support for years to come.

What can be learned from counselling adult adopted people? It should be remembered at this stage that only a very small percentage of all those adopted come for counselling. They show, however, that the 'need to know' about oneself is a basic need, and social workers must therefore enable adoptive parents to explain the facts of adoption to children *as they grow up*. They must help the new parents understand the importance of keeping the channels of communication open so that the subject can be discussed and re-discussed openly. Social workers must obtain as much relevant information as possible about the child's birth family, including age, racial origin, physical and mental health, education, skills, interests, the circumstances of the placement and the history of the child from birth. Photos are invaluable as so often the adoptees say 'I just want to see what she looked like, I don't want to meet her'. Under the 1984 Adoption Rules all this information is required for the agency court report so it should also be in the agency record. Safe and systematic preservation of records must be a priority for every adoption agency. The birth parents too need to know that the file is not closed, and that he or she may be sought out in years to come.

It seems that, despite many developments towards 'openness', adopters still need help with 'explaining' about adoption. It may be assumed that in a more open society it is easier to talk about sex, illegitimacy and adoption but most adopters need practical help about how to tell – what words, what books or methods to use. There are still young children placed for adoption with no memory of their birth family, who depend entirely on information from their adoptive parents. It may be that we have not offered enough help or offered it at the right time, and perhaps there should be opportunities for adopters to talk to social workers years after the order has been made, through a positive follow-up from the agency rather than the informal 'come and see us anytime' approach. Many social workers have experienced working with adopted adolescents, going through a crisis at home, and wondered why the adopters didn't seek help earlier. Perhaps the help has *to be offered* at an earlier stage.

The issue of identity is fundamental. All children growing up away from their birth parents need to have a positive sense of who they are and where they have come from. It is to be hoped that the provision of photos of the birth family, the use of life story-books and guidance from social workers to the adopters, before and after the order, may meet the need of children currently being placed. The social worker is accountable to those children.

Counselling adult adopted people sometimes brings the counsellor face to face with a child they may have placed years ago: the adoption does not end when the order is made; the accountability extends to the adult adopted person. We have learnt all this, and are continually learning more.

THE CHILDREN'S SOCIETY, NORWICH
Elisabeth Traverse

'The child wants a home'
Our project opened in 1980 as 'The child wants a home', and aimed to find new families for children with special needs. Up to June 1987 we had placed 63 children. Of these, seven placements have disrupted and two babies with Down's syndrome have died. Many families have needed post-placement support and some have come back for post-adoption counselling.

By 1985 we had begun to focus our minds increasingly on what happens after legal adoption for all the parties concerned. We decided to do a six-month pilot study to test the need for post-adoption services in our area (Norfolk and North Suffolk). We felt the research of Macaskill[1] had already demonstrated the need for this support to be available for 'special needs' families, so we widened our pilot study so that it also included baby placements made by any agency.

We applied our test on four main fronts:
- the general public, for whom we held a public discussion meeting on 'Adoption and identity' and two open days
- other professionals, for whom we provided adoption awareness work in the form of a workshop for teachers and liaison with child guidance staff and Norfolk Social Services Department
- the voluntary sector, through liaison with Parent-to-Parent Inform-

ation on Adoption Services (PPIAS) and the National Organisation for the Counselling of Adoptees and Parents (NORCAP)
– other agencies and research findings.

Test results

The *public meeting* was attended by 13 people, two of whom were adopted teenagers in care. Two follow-on meetings were requested by those who attended. The *open days* were taken up by 15 callers, the majority of whom were adult adopted people working at identity issues. All those who responded were concerned with baby placements.

Professional workers and the *voluntary groups* were very encouraging about the need for a service and saw it as a useful addition to the work they were already doing. The flexible, non-statutory nature of our project was seen as valuable.

Studying the *research*, we were struck by two main themes:
– no one has so far found a way to measure 'successful' adoptions
– 'transplanting' a child is not yet fully understood from all emotional viewpoints of the 'adoption triangle' (adopters, adopted people and birth parents).

Also, we were aware of the debates between researchers, notably Raynor[2] and Haimes and Timms,[3] as to why adopted people seek information about, and in some cases try to trace, their birth family.

Based on the findings of our pilot study, we have drawn up the following list of aims:

1 to study in depth the idea of 'transplanting' the child, from the viewpoint of the adoption triangle, and to add to the body of knowledge available
2 to continue to experiment with services for the public and to develop these further
3 to develop 'adoption awareness' work with more professionals and the general public
4 to include the not-unrelated subject of artificial insemination by donor (AID) in our work
5 to amass statistics and case histories in order to publicise the need for services and to press for the necessary funding to be forthcoming from the public sector
6 to work under a research banner (University of East Anglia)
7 to produce relevant audio/visual and reading matter.

Since our pilot study, we have continued our initiatives by running a series of meetings on various aspects of adoption and on our availability to counsel, publicised by posters and in the media. We have started to hold monthly open days, which have so far been used mostly by adopted people and birth parents. We have run a successful workshop exploring how to help children with mental handicaps to understand the idea of adoption, and workshops for local authority social workers and trainee GPs on adoption awareness. The latter is intended to include AID awareness. For the education authority, we have agreed to organise a series of four study sessions on 'Separation, loss and rejection', and to produce written material on adoption for teachers. We have established a telephone contact register for adopters of 'special needs' children, having gleaned names from PPIAS and other agencies. We have run three public discussion meetings on 'Adoption and identity' and a workshop on communicating adoption to young children. All events have been well attended. As well as continuing these initiatives, we are about to run a meeting on step-parent adoption and hold a day workshop for transracial adopters and their children.

The particular challenges

Few adoptive parents use the open day service, but they do attend workshops and meetings. Our experience of this lack of interest in direct counselling is borne out elsewhere (notably Barnardo's Scottish Telephone Advice Service)[4] and is reflected in the research of Raynor.[5] We want to experiment with and evaluate different ways of trying to reach adopters of all types of children. We need to find out more about how they feel, what services they want, how to attract them without invading their privacy and questioning their right to be parents in their own manner.

Also pressing is the question of how we fund what must be established in time as a national preventive service. At present post-adoption support is largely a 'feeding on demand' service for families, often involved only at the intractable problem stage. Families need a service they can call on at any time and certainly while the problems can still be resolved within the family. For this to be available, the issue of funding is crucial.

References

1 Macaskill C 'Post-adoption support: is it essential?' *Adoption & Fostering* 9 1 1985.

2 Raynor L *The adopted child comes of age* Allen and Unwin, 1980.

3 Haimes E and Timms N *Adoption, identity and social policy* Gower, 1985.

4 Lindsay M and McGarry K 'Scottish Adoption Advice Service Report' Barnardo's (Scotland) 1984.

5 See 2 above.

LOTHIAN REGION SOCIAL WORK
Gerry O'Hara

Developing post-placement support services in Lothian:
A. The agency response

Lothian Region is the second largest Scottish regional authority (population approximately 800,000) and has a well documented and specific child care policy. Substitute family care was reorganised in the early 1980s into either time-limited, task-oriented fostering or permanent parenting. In permanent placements, whether adoption or fostering, the intention was that families 'assume a full parental role'.[1] The Social Work Department's policy was to work to an explicit target: that no child under 12 should remain in care for more than two years and that, if rehabilitation to the natural family was not possible, then the child should be resettled in a permanent home and, unless otherwise indicated, that the permanent home should be an adoptive one. The main implications of this policy are that:

– the great majority of children with real bonds to their natural families are, as a result of more directive planning, returned home within short time-scales

– a large proportion of children are placed in adoptive homes although some are placed on a foster-care basis intended to be permanent. In the five years since permanency planning was accepted by the Regional Council as part of its child care policy, the number of children in care has reduced by approximately one half.

'Time of change' (Lothian Region 1981)[2] was a clear commitment to close a number of children's homes and transfer resources to developing a range of community services for children. The homefinding team was established in order to place the children who had been in care for some time, as well as those who were continuing to be referred for permanent placement. Whilst local area teams were to be involved in placing younger children in permanent homes, the brief of the homefinding team was to find and make permanent placements for special needs children. Broadly speaking their aims and objectives were to recruit, prepare and assess families offering permanent new homes to special needs children and to support such placements. Specifically, the brief included a commitment to develop a post-placement support service that would be used by both adopters and foster parents who had taken children on a permanent basis.

This chapter is an attempt to describe briefly the progress made with the development of post-placement support services.

Post-placement support services available and being developed

Lothian's child care strategy[3] states that 'new families will have the right to such aftercare assistance from the Social Work Department as they require to integrate the child into the new community'. From this it can be supposed that both post-placement and post-adoption work is a part of the adoption service. In fact, although post-placement work is general practice, post-adoption work is still patchy. However, in 1985 the Department accepted the following principles:

– the need to support adoptive families both up to and after, if necessary, the granting of an adoption order
– the need to develop opportunities for families both from within our own agency and from other agencies with specialist skills and understanding of older child adoption to be involved in post-adoption support
– recognition that the consumer self-help group which the adoption team has encouraged (Lothian Adopters' Group – see below) is of crucial importance, in partnership with us, in developing support services
– acknowledgement of the work done by some of the key people in the Lothian Adopters' Group by paying them for direct family and groupwork support on a sessional basis
– commitment to examining, in the longer term, funding for a paid counsellor/secretary, who should also be an adoptive parent, to be employed by the Lothian Adopters' Group
– primary responsibility for developing a post-adoption service to be held by Lothian's specialist homefinders, and for this to be relevant to both local area need and the adopters themselves.

Specifically and in detail what we actually offer to families is as follows:

1 Every family is supported by their social worker and often the child's social worker up to the time of the granting of the adoption order.
2 The family's social worker usually offers a crisis intervention service, post adoption, if the adoptive family require this.
3 There is a range of support/training groups available to adoptive families, run in co-operation with the adopters themselves – sometimes with direct social work involvement, often not.
4 We are attempting to develop a service for adopters in co-operation with colleagues at the Department of Child and Family Psychiatry at the Royal Hospital for Sick Children in Edinburgh. This is proving extremely successful with growing co-operation, although there is a need for more work to be done with other agencies offering counselling services to families in the community.
5 Finally, and most importantly, the partnership with the Lothian Adopters' Group offers a clear and structured peer group support network that will contribute to the development of the whole range of adoption services in Lothian Region.

The partnership with Lothian Adopters' Group
The Lothian Adopters' Group was set up in March 1982 to assist the Department with the recruitment of families. It has grown, particularly in the last two years, to a sizeable and important group. Currently there are over 100 families involved in one way or another. The range of activities on offer includes:
– monthly general support meeting
– counselling service for adopters, by adopters with specialist skills (e.g. a clinical psychologist and trained counsellors)
– range of post-placement training groups for adopters at different stages
– 'listening ear' service
– babysitting service
– the development of a financial structure to allow families to be given help in a variety of ways (e.g. grants to allow children to be sent on adventure holidays to give families respite or grants to help with private tutoring where children are under-achieving)

- monthly newsletter which keep adopters in touch with one another
- advice, consultation and active participation with the Social Work Department, recruiting and preparing families and children for adoption and permanent fostering.

Whilst we accept the evidence from various studies that families adopting special needs children are faced with often intractable problems requiring in some cases 'forever support', it has to be acknowledged that in a large local authority, despite the commitment of specialist workers, it would not be realistic for the agency to offer the bulk of the support directly. We believe that encouraging adopters to accept responsibility for developing their own support services is of fundamental importance, as well as being the most realistic and sensible way forward for us. The specialist homefinders in Lothian, some of whom are team-based social workers, can offer specific crisis intervention work with adoptive families who ask for such a service. This should not be underestimated because many of our adopters, particularly those who have been involved with the homefinding team in the last four years, have come back for such a service. However, the ongoing 'nuts and bolts maintenance' and training of families to cope with their adopted children is being developed by the adopters themselves, in partnership and in consultation with the adoption workers. Groupwork, which offers both general support and specific training for families at different stages, is happening and being developed. We are running a 12-session course on parenting skills for our most experienced adopters. This course is led by both social workers and parents and is aimed at supporting, sustaining and nurturing adopters and suggesting new parenting skills to these parents who, in the main, are responsible for not only the development of the Lothian Adopters' Group but the ongoing training and support of new and recent adopters.

We have found that it is vital to have a small amount of money from the Department to pay adopters who are involved in helping to run preparation groups and who offer specific help to other adopters. It puts a firm value on the skills and commitment of the adopters and it makes it easier for us to ask for their help. Similarly, families who receive help know that they are not just relying on the goodwill of their fellow adopter, but that this is part of a thought-out developing service that is paid and professionally supported. We have found that the most active members of the Lothian Adopters' Group themselves need a good deal of consultation. We have had to work out a Code of Practice on issues of confidentiality. When the adopters' group has had to intervene with the Department to advocate on behalf of a family, we have had to accept in as mature and trusting a way as possible our different perceptions. This has not always been easy but a partnership which was merely collaborative and which did not respect the difference between a large local authority with a professional adoption service and a strong consumer group would, we believe, stunt the growth and independence of the group.

Our most recent plan is to use part of a vacant homefinder post to provide the money to employ a secretary for the parents' group to further develop the service. The effect in Lothian of an adoption service that is consumer-influenced from the recruitment stage, right the way through, has been dramatic. The reason that the specialist team feel able to give up part of one of their posts is because they know that they will get so much more back by using it to employ a secretary in this way. It is an enormous relief not to be the 'all wise worker', and to acknowledge that special needs adoption is still new, with many unanswered questions about the cost to families and the outcome for children. We should throw away some of our 'tablets of stone', listen to what consumers want and make a start at a real partnership.

References

1 McKay M 'Planning for permanent placement' *Adoption & Fostering* 9, 1 1980.

2 Lothian Regional Council 'Time of change' (A review of residential provision for children and young people) 1981.

3 McKay M 'The need for permanent families' paper presented at a seminar 'Children in care' Lothian Regional Council 1981.

Developing post-placement support services in Lothian:
B. Setting up the adopters' group
Douglas Hutton

Lothian Adopters' Group (LAG) is an adopters' support group attached to the adoption homefinding team in the Lothian Region Social Work Department. Four years ago there was no active group. Today LAG has links with around 100 families. As there is now a growing recognition of the value of this type of group, but at the same time considerable uncertainty as to how support groups can be established, the conception, birth and early development of this group may be of some general interest.

Before any adopters' group has a chance of success it must have reasonably unhindered access to its agency, which in turn is possible only if there is genuine respect and co-operation between the adopters and the social workers jointly initiating the venture. This perhaps appears obvious – I mention it only because it is likely to remain for most co-operative ventures the greatest obstacle, as it was in Lothian seven or eight years ago. At the time, to childless couples like my wife and myself, the adoption service seemed to be in a state of crisis due to the shortage of babies for adoption. We learned that children's homes were packed with school-age children and that many of these children needed new families, but that this was regarded by many as extremely risky. We were willing to take the risk but were frustrated by the slowness of the Social Work Department to adapt its service to the new situation. The result was mutual mistrust and antagonism which came to a head when we eventually did succeed in having older children placed with us. By this time we were only too keen to dismiss the agency's tentative offers of post-placement support and to rely entirely on our own resources. We were, however, in a lonely place with the knowledge that many years of difficulties with the children were still to unfold. We later found that our embattled situation was not unusual for families in our position. Because there was little experience around of older adoptive placements, we would not trust our workers' judgements. They too lacked confidence in themselves and in us. There was little common ground. From our defensive position workers could be threatening, interfering, patronising, inefficient and negligent.

So when LAG took root four years ago this marvellous spirit of co-operation which I started to describe was non-existent. LAG came about as a result of a meeting we had with Gerry O'Hara, who had just been appointed to run Lothian's adoption service. We were there in the knowledge that hundreds of children in care of the Region could be considered for adoption but that very little was happening. The gist of our case was that the adoption service would be best run by those who knew something about adoption – namely the adopters. To our surprise Gerry O'Hara took us on, giving us a part to play in the publicity campaign which he was about to organise for the recruitment of more adoptive families. We invited other adopters to help and we soon had an adopters' group of six or seven couples.

The original group was highly motivated and full of enthusiasm. We had been given a clear brief to evangelise about adoption and we warmed to the task with missionary zeal. We were also being recognised – perhaps we adopters have an unusual need for recognition – and, most important of all, our authority as parents was being acknowledged. We all gave the impression of being very successful. Failure was almost unthinkable and support, other than in trivial practical matters, quite unnecessary.

One consequence of this gathering of experienced adopters at a time of recruitment, followed by intense activity in preparation and placements on an unprecedented scale, was that some members of the group, ourselves included, went on to adopt further children. As we were organisers of the group, there followed a brief hiatus in its activities as we re-adjusted our personal priorities. LAG was dormant for about a year. When it re-assembled about three years ago, it was as a ginger group to encourage further adoptions of school-age children. Monthly meetings were re-established as a focus for the group's activities. For several months attendances were low and we began to wonder if we still had any role. In our frustration we talked to each other in the group about our own circumstances, partly from curiosity but mainly to pass the time. We began to drop our defences and to develop quite close friendships. Before long we were in deep discussions about our own needs as well as our children's – our problems of understanding, discipline, neighbours, family reactions, schools and our exhaustion at times. Most frequent topics were – and still are – our children's behaviour and our control over them. Consciously or unconsciously we had developed such uncompromising regimes to cope with the difficulties presented by our children that most people, including prospective adopters we met through LAG, found our revelations of our own family lives quite unpalatable. This sort of reaction and incomprehension of our day-to-day living has made us value even more the understanding of our peers in LAG. Even within the group there are wide differences of attitude and perception which can be related as much as anything else to the stage of placement: this must be a primary consideration when members are matched to meet for support.

For a long time we had clung to the idea that post-adoption support was necessary for beginners and for social workers but that we were beyond that stage. Our self-sufficiency seemed to depend on denying the possibility that we might at some time need support. We finally had to face our own frailty when some of the long-standing members stopped coming to meetings and we found the reason was that their placements had disrupted, not after a few months but after three or four years. We knew we were close enough to the same place, without however being sure what margin remained. What shocked us almost as much was to realise that LAG had little to offer adopters who were near their limit and nothing at all to offer families after disruption. It was soon obvious that all of us older adopters were under serious stress for much of the time. More of the pretending stopped and further barriers came down.

When we now look back to where we began in LAG, we realise that we have made a complete U-turn in our attitude to support. We all need support, or easy access to support, for many years after adopting our children. We have also changed our concepts of success and failure. We are more aware of the need to support families in crisis and after breakdown; with LAG members who have some experience of counselling in such situations, we are now more confident that we have sufficient credibility to be of some value here.

For the past three years LAG has had a constitution and an Annual General Meeting. Office bearers are elected, but strict adherence to formalities has never been an issue, which is perhaps as well as the management structure is in a constant state of change due to the rapid growth of the group and its changing needs. The Secretary is co-ordinator of group discussions and other acitivities and the main contact, principal counsellor and members' advocate when the need arises. There are various committees and working parties pursuing different goals in the interests of the members. The Social Work Department is represented on the committee which controls our finance, as we have a budget from the Region for our contribution to post-adoption support services. Our members are paid fees and expenses for formally-recognised support work although, in practice, only a small proportion of LAG's activity falls within this category.

The main forum is still the monthly meeting, which has attendances of up to around 30. There are invited speakers at about half of the meetings, and they usually attract large numbers. Whatever the agenda, most meetings turn into general discussions. The meeting and all other activities are reported in the monthly newsletter which is also used to float a few ideas about how LAG is developing. Referrals are taken from other adoption agencies and there is an 'adoption club' for children in care who are awaiting new families.

Finally, here in outline are some of our conclusions about the conditions which are helpful, if not essential, in setting up an adopters' group.

1 Adopters need the responsibility and the trust to organise their groups to suit themselves. It follows that they must then provide most of the initiative.

2 When the agency is part of a large authority, there is great advantage in having a specialist team with which the group can form close links. The concept of a partnership is clear only when each group – adopters and social workers – is clearly identified.

3 The support required is primarily for adopters as parents and for their parental authority. (Not all workers recognise this.)

4 The agency must recognise that adopters can give as much as they can receive. This two-way exchange should be the basis of the partnership and must be encouraged both formally and informally.

5 Geographical limits must be set so that members of the group can meet with reasonable convenience.

Developing post-placement support services in Lothian:
C. A personal view of the adopters' support group
Sandra Hutton

Over the years we in Lothian Adopters' Group have spent many hours trying to understand the nature of adoption. We have come to believe that there are two fundamental issues facing adopting families which mark us out as different from other kinds of carers. First, it is our task to take our children on their first real journey into the past. What we are working with, or more likely against, are the life-story books which tell us on pink paper, with flowers round the edge, that all the people who could not or would not look after our children are worthy in our eyes and have tried jolly hard. Our children know that two and two make four but they have learnt to humour us – to save us and them the painful bits. It is an unwelcome surprise for them to come across adults who are taking them in there, exposing the fantasies.

Second, all the time our children have been in care and have been moved around, they have been told that they have been in no way responsible for their behaviour. Worker after worker understands that our children could not help lying, stealing, having temper trantrums, showing aggression, being destructive. The children are right in there with that one. What a relief to dissociate yourself from all the things you did in anger or stress. The result is that our children have systematically and deliberately had taken away from them the only thing that has ever truly belonged to them – responsibility for their own actions. When our children come to us, they don't exist in their own minds and, left unchecked, can only grow into adults who don't know who they are. We have to develop new skills as parents, to bring into play the idea of responsibility, even in a bad situation.

We have our own difficulties. Since our children suffer from low self-esteem, they don't spend much of their time building us up as parents. As our self-image gets dented by our children, we need to be affirmed and regarded as having something to give. We need to be seen as pioneers, a polite term for guinea pigs. It is fundamental to the structure of our adopters' group that we receive, but we also give. We are valued by each other in our sharing of experience, and valued by the Social Work Department in being asked to co-lead a group or to contact a family in crisis.

The image-denting changes us. When the Social Work Department takes us on, we have our pride in being coping adults, in coping families, and we are ready for the challenge of living with a damaged child. The reality can be frightening. Our marriage relationships become strained as we blame each other when we are personally overstretched. We see our existing children display anxiety as they watch our coping level fall. But what distresses us most of all is to be regarded suddenly as a non-coping family instead of a family under stress which, if you think about it, is really very predictable. We don't need to be split up or given psychiatric help behind mirrors and we don't want our new children taken away for crude adjustment. We need help where we are, on the basis that something is bound to happen when a hurt child joins a family. In fact, if the family is working, that hurt ought to be showing. Nothing makes us madder than having our symptoms treated. In the adopters' group we like to know our helpers and we like to know they respect us.

The more we learn to love our children, the more it dawns on us that we can't cure emotional handicap. As more and more is demanded of us by our children at a deep level, so we have higher expectations of our helpers. We seem to meet two crisis times in adoption: about two years after placement when we begin to sense the depth of the hurt to our children and again two years later when we are felled by fear of the future and by fatigue. At these points other adopters can't take us because of the threatening things we are saying – our talk even frightens ourselves. At these lowest points we need experts to help us and to look at ways of alleviating the tiredness and stress. We also need the LAG worker's ear close to the ground to pick up our distress signals and to offer us the link to formal support because we will be overwhelmed and unable to make the slightest move. It may be difficult to understand that when we get in touch requesting help, we are actually in quite good fettle. Long silences can be a danger sign.

Adoption is about being boss of our kids, but it is an uncomfortable relationship because in the end the children hold the power. They have the trump card, which is to expose us as failures. Our children dice with death at an instinctive level but they haven't thought it through, so the control game is one we have to win for everyone's sake. What this boils down to is learning techniques to sustain our supremacy. We adopters talk endlessly to each other about day-to-day living. It is a common feeling that professionals would be shocked to spend real time in our homes observing the control struggles with our children and the lengths to which we go to win. When we talk to each other, we know the reality. We can share the truth, which is that we have had to resort to methods which would be repugnant in other circumstances. We believe that the level of placements holding together in our group is directly attributable to the working out of survival techniques. This sub-culture is shared with professionals sparingly, and only with those who we know will uphold us.

Put simply, the primary purpose of our support system is to maintain our authority. We are safe with each other in the adopters' group because we all know the difference between support and interference. When the group began, it was rife with stories of trying to deal with professionals who didn't know the difference. One of the best achievements of our partnership with the Social Work Department is having a successful mix of professional and lay help.

If our support system really works, it will give us permission to let our children go. We do not want to be held to our task beyond what is tolerable to us. The burden will have become intolerable if we have been unable to get our children to trust us, or if we have been unable to uncover their fantasies. We would define adoption as a bid for change. When we stop talking of change, we stop talking of adoption and start talking of despair. Our placements can cease to be worthwhile and release should be merciful. Perhaps the biggest achievement of all the work that has gone into the adopters' group, from both sides of the partnership, is the recognition that adoption is not necessarily an end in itself.

We are on a journey with our children but essentially it is their journey and it will not always be appropriate for us to be with them all the way. If we have begun to address the issue of responsibility and have introduced the concept of choice, then that may have been good enough. Most adopters struggle to find and accept that base-line but, once it is reached, the children have the conditions which allow them to be people in their own right.

WANDSWORTH SOCIAL SERVICES
Pauline Dancyger and Mary Griffiths-Jones

In Wandsworth our first post-adoption groups were set up in 1968 and continued until 1976. The aims were to enable adopters to share their experiences, good and bad, to talk about any particular difficulties and to support each other. It was an opportunity for social workers both to learn from families and to offer a service to adopters. It also provided a forum for people to ask for further information about their children. Meetings took place on a weekday evening in a room in the municipal buildings. They were held regularly throughout the year and an average of eight couples were invited to each group meeting. The groups were divided according to the age of the adopted child in the family.

Between the years of 1976 and 1985 a variety of support services were arranged for different groups of adopters. For black families who had already adopted, and for families who expressed an interest in either long-term fostering or adoption, annual workshops were arranged. These workshops were well attended and much enjoyed by everyone, and proved an excellent way of finding new families.

In 1981 a support group for black adopters and long-term foster parents was set up in the adoption unit by our black families homefinding worker. Through her work with the black community she had recognised the need to offer black families something separate from the larger, mixed adoption and fostering groups. This group continued until 1985, with between eight and ten families meeting, initially fortnightly, and subsequently monthly. This is now an independent self-supporting group of people who no longer need formal leadership.

In 1983 a further post-adoption support group was set up for families with children aged nine to eleven years, the majority of whom turned out to be transracial adopters.

Support for transracial adopters

Although we in Wandsworth had arranged post-adoption meetings for families with children of particular ages, nothing specifically aimed at transracial adopters was arranged until 1985 when, because of widespread media coverage of this issue, we felt it was important to offer a meeting to such parents. We wanted to share our thinking about same-race placements, find out the families' views about current developments and offer support if needed.

The first meeting was held in October 1985. It was difficult to identify all transracial placements from our statistics but we were able to invite 45 families, twelve of whom attended. The meeting took place on Saturday with a shared lunch, a panel discussion and small discussion groups. Black and white staff were present and there was advice on skin and hair care and a multi-racial bookstall. The day gave families the opportunity to air their views, share their concerns and, very importantly, a chance for their children to get together. It became clear that these families had very different needs. Those living in white suburban areas had other concerns than those living in inner city areas, and there were the differing needs of Asian and Afro-Caribbean children.

After this day the families who had attended, along with some who had not been able to be there, expressed an interest in an annual meeting and a support group to meet regularly for those living close to the Borough. This support group began to meet in 1986 and was very much involved in planning and arranging the second day for transracial adopters. Again it was apparent within the support group that transracial adopters do not necessarily share the same concerns. The ages of children, their personalities and whether or not the black child was the only adopted child in the family, made a difference. Among the issues discussed were helping the children to develop a positive racial

51

identity, education and combating prejudice in the community. Input from a sympathetic black worker was very welcome. We have in Wandsworth a group of black workers who are willing to help in any way possible.

The second day for transracial adopters was held in October 1986 and was more relaxed and informal than the first. This time ten families met together with black and white staff and the children were able to renew acquaintances from the previous year. The day was felt to be a success, partly because it was organised by adopters themselves, and partly because the families were feeling less defensive and were really committed to seeking constructive help for themselves and their children. They seemed aware of their responsibilities in bringing up black children within a white family and in a white society. A black social worker led the discussion group which followed lunch.

The result of the day was that families who came were keen to continue to meet annually and, where possible, to become part of a regular support group, meeting every other month. There was an urgent need to meet black families who had adopted and to share experiences with them. One suggestion was that the support group could be broadened to include black families.

Current plans
Apart from the black and transracial groups, it has been agreed to restart a group for all approved adopters. This will be an open group and will allow people to join automatically following their approval by the adoption panel. It will also be open to any adopters Wandsworth has approved in the distant past, as well as to more recent adoptive families.

It is clear that many families do want continuing contact and are prepared to put energy into developing this valuable resource, from which social workers involved in the tasks of finding permanent families can also learn so much.

AN ESSEX INITIATIVE
Alex Cunningham and Monty Cohen

In 1985 a mini-crisis occurred in one of our adoptive families because of their young child's sexual precocity. Her behaviour, stemming from her pre-placement experiences, suggested possible sexual abuse, and in helping her and the adopters to deal with this problem we became aware of the need for a post-adoption service.

Accordingly we obtained permission (though no extra staff hours) to initiate a voluntary post-adoption scheme in our area with the ambitious goals of enabling families:
- to handle more effectively a child's behaviour and other problems
- to handle emotive and perhaps inappropriate attitudes of the adopters or the child to pre-adoptive experiences and relationships
- to assist the child to achieve a positive self-image and identity in the long term through an acceptance of his or her origins
- to share experiences and knowledge gained with other adoptive families facing similar difficulties.

Staff from our local child guidance clinic expressed their interest in providing specialist help as they were already seeing a disproportionate number of adopted children, especially those experiencing identity problems in adolescence, in their daily work.

We sent out a brief questionnaire to survey the need for a post-adoption service and an invitation to a planning meeting, to about 20 families in our area who had recently adopted a child. Of the fifteen couples who responded, twelve wanted to participate. Most of them favoured occasional group meetings, while a few wanted an informal telephone network and two or three couples saw a need for individual or family counselling sessions or even referral to specialists. The general feeling seemed to be that, whilst they did not wish to be continually reminded of their adoptive status, families would welcome a safety-net in case of troubled times ahead. Letting the group dictate the manner in which we proceeded, we agreed that the service would include:
- an informal telephone network, with families being linked only over specific issues and after their permission had been sought
- support for new applicants, if required, from experienced adopters to

---

This article was first published in *Adoption & Fostering* in 1985. Since publication the post-adoption service has not developed formally but the families continue to meet socially twice a year. The local authority has fourteen area offices and counselling is available to adopters and adoptees on request.

help them combat the anxieties aroused by assessment and legal procedures, pre-placement blues or post-placement doubts
- half-yearly 'social' meetings, to include the children (as adopters had been impressed by the 'caring and sharing' attitude of adopted children towards each other at Parent-to-Parent Information on Adoption Services garden parties). Adopters agreed to take it in turns to act as hosts, since it was felt that using our office as a venue inhibited free discussion.

So far, only the third alternative above has attracted real interest. Two purely social gatherings have been held, each attended by about seven families. The children present have been very similar in age (toddlers to six year olds), and this had been a bonus as they get on well together. Some of these families keep in touch with each other between meetings, providing mutual support and an informal network of information on local facilities. At least one parent could see the advantage of the children growing up as friends, thus facilitating spontaneous discussions with peers of their feelings about adoption. New adoptive parents are automatically invited to join this group and some meet old acquaintances from the preparatory groups sessions we run twice a year for new applicants.

Two years on, we feel that an adequately staffed post-adoption service is required to help families:

1 explain adoption to a child and so deal constructively with
- the adults' feelings, if infertile, about acting as substitute parents
- the child's feelings of rejection by the birth parents, and possible self-hate
- the family's attitude towards the child's origins, including unpalatable facts about child abuse, serious neglect, or other problems in the background

2 handle access problems concerning
- the child who may be finding it difficult to relate to two sets of parents and have divided loyalties[1]
- the child's natural relatives, including perhaps the birth parents (who need to accept the role of 'distant relative' rather than that of custodial parent),[2] siblings, or extended family members with whom the child has had significant relationships
- previous caretakers, including foster parents with whom strong attachments exist, or other adoptive families who have adopted the child's siblings

- the exchange of photographs, cards, gifts, if this has not ended with the making of the adoption order
3 cope with behaviour problems in the child and learn more effective responses, especially to sexual promiscuity or delinquent behaviour which adoptive parents sometimes feel must be through inherited tendencies
4 help each other and new adopters in an informal self-support group.
Post-adoption counselling and similar self-support groups could also be of benefit to:
- step-families and natural extended families who are having difficulty in working out access issues and new relationships with the child in family adoptions
- adult adopted people who are trying to seek their families of origin and, later, in the post-honeymoon period of reunion
- birth parents who have relinquished their children for adoption (whether voluntarily or not), especially at vulnerable periods like Christmas and anniversaries.

References

1 Holmans A 'Exclusive and inclusive concepts of fostering' in Triseliotis J (ed), *New developments in foster care and adoption*, Routledge & Kegan Paul, 1980.

2 Adcock M 'Alternatives to adoption' *Adoption & Fostering* 8 1 1984.

PARENTS FOR CHILDREN
Hedi Argent

Parents for Children has been placing children with special needs for adoption for ten years. The agency has always offered regular support to families after they have adopted and in addition a worker to develop and take responsibility for a comprehensive post-adoption service was appointed in August 1985.

The aim of the Parents for Children post-adoption service is to offer the continuing support adoptive families have said they want. Whenever and wherever possible this means making the most of existing provisions rather than creating new services. For instance, local authority adopters' groups or groups concerned with specific disabilities are being encouraged to include Parents for Children families. In return, the Parents for Children post-adoption worker is able to offer joint training sessions or speakers for local authority groups and departments, or for other voluntary agencies. The eight segments of the Parents for Children post-adoption service are described here.

1 Regional groups

A study of half of the Parents for Children adoptive families by Catherine Macaskill in 1983/4 demonstrated a need for locally-based support groups.[1] As a result the families who have so far adopted through Parents for Children were divided into ten regional groups, there was one general meeting for all the families to discuss the reorganisation of the post-adoption service and each regional group had met by the end of 1986. Some have held a series of meetings.

It is too early to predict whether regional groups will become the most effective way to service adoptive families. It is already clear that many Parents for Children families welcome this form of support after they have adopted their children and prefer it to six-monthly or annual home visits, the previous practice. They like to meet each other and do not feel obliged to be the hosts or to feel responsible for what is said, even if we meet in one of their own homes. Generally the meetings are held in local halls and everyone brings and shares coffee, lunch and tea. The children are welcome and there is always time and a corner to speak privately to the Parents for Children worker if desired – but no one has to. Some families undoubtedly do miss having their own worker to themselves and this will have to be evaluated in due course.

Different groups have expressed different interests and shown different capacities. Some have undertaken projects such as finding a family who will offer respite care to their adopted children with handicaps, or putting pressure on their education authority to provide a domiciliary speech therapist. One group has organised a circulation scheme of half a dozen journals, and two groups are becoming involved in the recruitment and preparation of further adoptive families. New families are invited to regional meetings and do not have to wait until the adoption has gone through.

So far the groups are relying a great deal on the Parents for Children specialist worker but it is hoped that they will become more autonomous and make links with other existing local groups and agencies so that eventually Parents for Children will service rather than organise the group activities. For the time being an annual meeting is being held in each region and the groups may, or may not, meet in between! Many families are keeping in touch with each other within the regions.

2 Telephone link service
This service has also grown out of the families' own suggestions. Two thirds of all the families have asked to be included in the telephone linking scheme so far. Each family describes itself and gives details of the services it uses on a simple form. All the forms are alphabetically filed in an attractive loose-leaf folder so that pages can be added or removed as families wish. Although families are often reluctant to make the first move, several of them have used the available contacts after initial encouragement from the Parents for Children worker.

3 Black to black
Parents for Children has placed several older black children and black children with handicaps in white families. One of the aims of the post-adoption service is to find black families to befriend them. So far we have linked four black families with white adoptive parents and their black children. Of course, some white adopters already had black friends, but others have welcomed these new friends and one mother has told us that the friendship has been the most important single factor in their son's successful adoption. Another mother has written to us:

'As white parents of four black children, we did not worry in the early days of parenting about not having any black friends: forming a loving secure relationship was the first priority. When we did feel the need, our isolated, rural position made it very difficult to find anyone, so we were delighted when Parents for Children came up with someone specially interested in helping families such as ours – someone West Indian, also with four children. They came to spend the day with us, and from that day came lots of help and direction.

We had never heard our children talking to other black children about their experiences as black people amongst whites. Although we feel their hurts with them, we could see there was relief for them in talking to those experiencing it for themselves – the need for sympathy *and advice from fellow sufferers, as against Mum and Dad, hadn't hit us before.*

One of our children said, "You are more black than us because your Mum and Dad are black". We were saddened that there seemed to be a sense of superiority in being 'less black'. Our new friends suggested practical ways to help ours think of themselves as 'black' rather than 'less black' – e.g. having a West Indian newspaper regularly, through which pen-pals could be arranged. We could see that having some black peers would help. To hear our children admiring the handsome looks and beautifully groomed hair of these other children was delightful – that for once they could admire their own sort of hair rather than envy ours must be good.

Our eldest daughter's hair was beautifully cornrowed during the day, thus giving Mum a valuable lesson. We were introduced to a far better comb – a little detail, but of enormous help. We discussed skin care as well and all help was sensitively given with no sense of criticism of our own attempts.

The subject of West Indian food was raised and our children seemed very dubious. We were given the title of a new book to introduce us to the subject. We had never felt we needed to go into this area before, but being with this family made us think our children may be at a disadvantage, perhaps later, if they are totally ignorant on this subject.

At the end of the day, we felt we had a lot of work to do in helping our children appreciate their identity as they approach adolescence. Having the continuing support of this family, with whom we had so much in common straight away, gives us great encouragement and practical help.'

Parents for Children is increasing its efforts to seek black parents for black children, but in the meantime we hope that black families will continue to befriend the children who have been transracially placed for adoption.

4 Individual contacts

Although the post-adoption service is aimed at offering group support, contact with individual families remains an important part of the work. The Parents for Children post-adoption worker has telephone contact with an average of five families a week. These contacts vary from a five-minute telephone conversation in response to a practical query or routine call to keep in touch, to a 45-minute telephone disussion about an adoption problem.

One parent who rang recently left a message for the worker to say that there was nothing wrong but she needed to recharge her batteries. It took half an hour of listening and commenting on the progress obviously being made to recharge them. Home visits are rare but do happen. Sudden changes in family circumstances may need immediate and individual attention. Sickness, adolescence and renewed contact with a birth family have been recent reasons for visits and adopters, adoptees and birth parents are always welcome at the office.

5 Residential weekends
After an experimental residential weekend five years ago, several Parents for Children families expressed a wish for an annual residential event. The Parents for Children post-adoption service worker found a suitable venue and speakers in 1986, and one of the families organised the weekend with the help of the willing Parents for Children secretaries and the photocopier. In 1987 the whole event was organised by a single parent who had adopted twins with multiple disabilities and planning for the following year has already begun.

6 Workshop and discussion days
Parents for Children has always offered discussion days and workshops to all adoptive families. These events, which encourage the formation of interest groups, have now been included in the post-adoption service in addition to the regional groups. It is therefore possible for a family to belong to a group of parents who are coping with, for example, difficult adolescents, to attend three workshops during the year on a variety of topics (chosen by the families themselves), and to be members of their own local Parents for Children group – which may be linked to other services.

There is always an annual summer picnic, a social occasion for adoptive families, prospective adopters, relations, friends and neighbours.

7 Adoption awareness
It is the aim of the post-adoption service to encourage existing parent groups and service agencies to increase their awareness of the needs of adoptive families, for example:
– some adoptive parents of children with Down's syndrome have not

always felt welcome to join their local Down's Children's Association. The post-adoption worker wrote an article which was published in the Down's Children Association newsletter and was followed by a feature of edited comments from the adoptive parents themselves

– links have been established with the Tavistock clinic in North London in order to explore the special needs of adoptive families: referrals can now be quickly taken up by the clinic.

8 Evaluation

It is necessary to evaluate what we are doing before we do more of it. A special grant enabled a researcher to begin a three-month study during 1987. So far, the only evaluation has come from families. One parent said 'Now that I know there's a service just for us, I don't mind taking up your time. Before, I always felt I was stopping another child being placed.'

Conclusion

The Parents for Children post-adoption service keeps in touch with every one of our adoptive families: this means of course that confidentiality has to be examined and explained. What kinds of records should we keep after adoption and for what purpose? There are many questions still to be answered. In the meantime, we are offering this service as a right and not a favour: the expectation of post-adoption support is therefore built into the preparation for adoption. While the families use the service, the agency learns about what works and what does not, from the only people who know.

References

1 Macaskill C 'Post-adoption support: is it essential?' *Adoption & Fostering* 9 1 1985 and 'Who should support after adoption' *Adoption & Fostering* 9 2 1985.

THE INDEPENDENT ADOPTION SERVICE
Joan de Silva

The experience of finding families for older special needs children over the past ten or so years has highlighted for the Independent Adoption Service (IAS) the long-term nature of this work. We have always maintained contact with our adoptive families: this was demonstrated when some of the children adopted during our very first year attended the agency's twenty-first birthday celebrations in September 1986. We have also kept in touch through the annual summer party which, while primarily a social occasion, also provides the opportunity for adults – both families and staff – to get together to exchange news and developments. Our tradition for adoptive families to be involved in the running of the agency by serving on the Management Committee and adoption panels provides an additional continuing link with adopters and their concerns.

However, as the characteristics of the children needing families become more complex and the number of IAS families increases, so the need for a post-adoption service which is supportive without being undermining, which is available as of need and right, and which does not come into play only in times of crisis and emergency, becomes increasingly apparent.

Having obtained a grant from a charitable trust, we began in 1986 to give some real attention to post-adoption work in its own right. We planned, within a two-year period, to establish a network of IAS families who might be interested in, and might benefit from, the opportunity of meeting together to discuss common issues and shared experiences. We recognised that a major change in the way placements have developed over the last ten years has been from transracial to same-race families, and we were concerned that the issues this raised could be explored. The work has been organised and co-ordinated by a post-adoption worker who has concentrated exclusively on post-adoption work, leaving the homefinding team free to work on recruitment and placement issues.

It was decided that the first group of families contacted would be those with whom older children had been placed from care during the years 1980 to 1985. These – 101 in all – were sent a questionnaire to ask their views.

The initial response was rather sparse but the information trickled in, both from families with whom the agency's social workers were still in contact and from those with whom contact had dwindled over the passage of time. The issues raised fell into four clear areas:
– contact with birth families
– support for children who had been sexually abused and for their adoptive families

- concern for adopted adolescents
- support for children and families where placements have been made transracially.

One of these, the question of support for sexually-abused children and their families, was already given priority in the agency's work both pre- and post-placement by individual counselling and in workshops set up to support parents bringing up children with particularly distressing life experiences such as non-accidental injury and neglect.

Another of the issues – further information about birth parents – was a concern of the majority of families who responded. The importance placed on obtaining and dealing with information about birth parents and life-story work for the children adopted as babies has led the post-adoption worker to be involved in three 'telling' workshops. These are now included as an automatic component of the agency's services to parents in the period following adoption. Another development emerging from this has been workshops for older children and their families, particularly when the child's history includes difficult information which may need to be expanded and explained further as the child grows older.

In recent months, four young adult adoptees have been in touch with a view to tracing their parents, and nine birth mothers have been in touch either to enquire about their children or to leave information about their current whereabouts. Having placed nearly 1,000 children during its 21 years, IAS is aware that it will face an increasing demand for counselling and advice of this sort from young adult adopted people seeking birth records and other information and from birth parents. As yet, it is impossible for us to estimate just how much time and effort may be involved in this work but we do know that long-established adoption agencies have found it to be considerable.

We have begun our post-adoption project with one part-time experienced and qualified worker, but we envisage the need for more staff and have prepared an outline plan for more workers as a 'placement support team'. In the meantime, the existing worker has backing and supervision from a special interest group consisting of the director, three workers and the administrative secretary, who has been with the agency for 20 years and is a considerable source of useful information. Additionally the worker will collaborate with staff in other agencies where post-adoption services are also being developed. We are aware that we are still in the early stages of what is likely to develop into a considerable service. We expect to co-operate with workers from other agencies, as well as with the families themselves, to achieve maximum results and to avoid duplication of effort.

4 Black children in black families

This chapter discusses post-placement work with black families. It raises interesting questions about the validity or relevance of legal adoption, as it is practised in Britain, for older members of the Afro-Caribbean community.

WORKING WITH AFRO-CARIBBEAN FAMILIES AFTER
PLACEMENT
Joan Fratter

The observations and experiences recorded here are those of a small team of adoption and fostering social workers and of seven black adoptive and foster parents, whose comments are directly quoted.

Barnardo's London Division Homefinding Project, based at Barkingside in Essex, comprises six social workers (two of whom are Afro-Caribbean), a senior social worker and a project leader. In the six years since April 1981 we have placed 36 children of Afro-Caribbean or Anglo-Afro-Caribbean parentage with black families. With the exception of a mixed-parentage baby and two pre-school brothers, all the Afro-Caribbean children placed were at least six years old, with the oldest being sixteen. More than half of the children placed had been living, prior to joining their new family, in one of Barnardo's prefostering and adoption units in 'The Village' and had been prepared to move on to a new family by the residential key worker. In April 1985 a Jamaican-born project worker was appointed to assist workers in the homefinding project and in the Village to prepare black children for placement with black families by increasing their knowledge and awareness of black identity and culture.

In considering post-placement support, we identified a number of areas or issues which seemed either specific to placements of black children with black families or different in degree or emphasis from the needs and experiences of white families. Inevitably race, culture and the experience of racism were key factors.

The child's awareness and acceptance of his or her black identity

'Black teenagers who have been brought up in care – they think differently. So there is a huge gap, not just a generation gap, but also a culture gap. But it's very important that we prepare the black child for living in a society that is racist.'

In almost every case there were concerns and difficulties when a child was placed with a black family. All the children, prior to placement, had been living with white caretakers, and most had not been cared for by a black adult since they had left their family of origin, often at a very early age. This led to children seeing themselves as white or brown, but not black:

'Maxine had obviously received some negative input about being black. She saw me very much as brown and she was quite pleased that she was with a brown person. She would actually say to me 'I'm glad I'm not living with them – they're black, aren't they'. She would burst into tears if I referred to her as black. She cried when I tried to plait her hair for school – she thought people would call her "nigger", so I had to leave her hair open.'

Some children had difficulty in accepting placement in a black family which they saw as inferior. One worker commented:

'I found it hard to believe – Marvin was black, blacker than I am, and yet he felt he was white. If you had put him with a white family he would probably have found it easier because he was totally white inside, a "coconut". Marvin called us a "black trash" family and his definition of black people was that they were muggers and thieves and they fill gaols.'

Marvin's attitude was formed not only by the lack of positive black models but because his mother also viewed white people as superior – she complained that her child had not been seen as 'good enough' to be placed with a white family.

It was hurtful to families to be abused by their foster children, and sometimes difficulties were created with relatives and friends:

65

'When Maxine began mixing with children who came from a background where they had been taught from an early age that they were black and it was okay to be black, her attitude caused problems between her and those children. At that age, eight or nine, it is an important issue.'

'A lot of black families just would not carry on when the child came calling them "nigger".'

Families found their own way of helping the child:

'When we first took Dwayne, I could see his attitude was as if he knew no other way than being with a white family. His attitude was that being with a black person was not the right way. In other words, he didn't think he was part of black society. So I had to sit with him and let him know that no matter how he looks upon himself he is still counted as a black person.'

'Actually it was only by taking Maxine to the West Indies, to Barbados, that she saw black people working in the banks, driving cars, etc. It took her a few weeks to get this together but she got a better perspective in Barbados of herself.'

'I went around and found black doctors and black teachers and I made an appointment with them and let Marvin have a chat with them and since I have done that he has never looked back about his colour and accepts that he is black. If I had not been prepared to do that then he would have lost his whole identity, which would have been sad.'

Although these families did not involve social workers directly in dealing with issues of identity, they stressed the important role of caretakers and social workers in preparing a child for placement:

'For black children really to survive with black families and to have respect for them their caretakers should be more educated about black people and their culture. If you are going to have one who does not really want to know anything about black, those children have lost the black community. My foster son did not feel that black people have any values.'

Families experiencing the hurtfulness of caring for a child who rejected his or her own identity found discussion with other families who had overcome this difficulty invaluable. Support could be offered either on an individual basis with families linked together by the social worker or through previously established contact in preparation groups or by discussion in post-placement meetings.

Some children felt more at ease in dealing with practical aspects, such as skin and hair care, once they were living in a black family:

'As for skin care, Maxine told me that staff made attempts to see to that, but because the oil in the water made the bath greasy, she always had to have her bath last and she felt ashamed – until she came to live with me. In the children's home, she never saw adults using cream on themselves. My friends used to ask Maxine to cream their babies' skin and so she came to see it as normal.'

In most cases, children who had initially found it difficult to adjust to living in a black family and to accept their black identity were eventually helped to do so, but in a few cases the problem persisted. One fifteen-year-old boy, born of Jamaican parents in the UK and received into care at the age of two, would not, a year after placement, walk alongside his Jamaican foster parents on family outings and refused to sit next to their relatives visiting from the West Indies. Attempts made to help Carl by a clinical psychologist and by the project worker were not successful.

The families' attitudes to adoption

'The word "adopt" is not in our vocabulary.'

In reflecting on the 36 placements made, a striking feature is that so few of the children have so far been adopted – a baby of Anglo-Afro-Caribbean parentage, a girl of ten (placed at the age of six) and two sisters aged six and seven at placement. This contrasts with the fact that of the 24 black children placed transracially before 1983, more than half have been adopted. The difference is accounted for partly by the age at which the group placed transracially joined their families (one third were under five) but in discussion several reasons were identified for the reluctance of black families to consider adoption rather than fostering:

a) *The concept of adoption*, as understood in Britain, with its secrecy and formality, is not part of the tradition of child care in the West Indies:

'*In the West Indies there would be no need to adopt a child to give them a sense of security – the child would know the relatives, the natural parents would know that the child was with that family. They would also have some input into that child's behaviour in that the "parent" could refer to the natural parent on any point of discipline. It would be very much a "loose" adoption. There is a permanency but there would be no need for formal adoption.'*

'*There is a saying in St Vincent: "This child is living with me but is not my own".'*

'*Quite honestly I never heard the word "adoption" before I came to England. If a family has maybe a lot of children and there is another family who feel they can provide for the child in a much better lifestyle, the child just lives with them and that's how it is and these people will just bring the child up as one of their own.'*

Some families had experienced pressure to adopt a child within a short time of placement. There was unease about why a social worker, in one instance, was pressing for adoption:

'*He was a bit pushy for adoption . . . It seemed like he was trying to get rid of the child to a certain extent. He didn't want to give an opportunity for a bond to be formed between the child and me.'*

Because many older black families do not share the widely-held view of adoption in this country – that it is more secure for the child and implies more commitment on the part of the new family than fostering – there was potential for misunderstanding and disagreement with social workers.

b) *Finance* was seen as a factor which deterred families both from coming forward as adopters and from adopting a child in their care:

'Adoption! You think straight away that people who want to adopt have got to have plenty of money.'

'In Britain black families earn much less than a white family, so therefore they cannot afford the upkeep of those children if they adopted them.'

'It would have been too expensive for me. There would be no income to support absences from work to give the child the extra care she needs. The fostering allowance isn't a hefty sum, but it's more than you get with adoption. I know they say when you adopt, the child becomes yours and you should be able to shoulder the financial burden, but that's different if you are well off and not a working-class parent living off your income.'

It seems that there is limited understanding among black families – as among families in general – about the availability of adoption allowances. Also, many schemes do not have sufficient flexibility regarding the amount of support which could be offered (for example, only the equivalent of the basic boarding out allowance may be payable, even for a child with a severe handicap or other special needs).

c) *The legal status in this country* of prospective adopters was seen as a factor which held people back:

'They themselves don't feel secure. They still think of the West Indies as "home" and every now and again some politician gets up and you hear about the activities of the National Front. I am in the process of getting a British passport which is going to cost me the earth because I need to know that at some point I am not going to be touched on the shoulder by the Immigration Law and sent back.'

It is sometimes difficult for white workers to acknowledge the impact of such anxiety on a family's sense of well-being and security.

d) *The motivation of black families* working with the project included, in many instances, a concern about the disproportionate number of black children in care and a wish to help parents who had tried to bring up their children in this country without the support of the extended family.

These families were rarely motivated by a wish to add to their family permanently through adoption and a comparison of the structure of the 42 families who had children placed with them between April 1984 and March 1986 (29 white families, 12 Afro-Caribbean families, one Asian) reveals that there was only one childless black family compared with ten white. Less than one third of the white families (nine) had children living at home, whereas more than half of the black families (seven) were caring for dependent children. More than three quarters of the black parents were over the age of 40 at the time of placement.

Although the figures quoted refer to a relatively small number of families, they do confirm the impression gained by project workers over the years that black families, having raised their own children to adulthood, or to a less dependent stage, were keen to offer a home to a child as a contribution towards helping her or him return to the black community. This 'inclusive' attitude towards caring for a child enabled many families, particularly in the older age group, to feel relaxed about the child having contact with her or his family of origin:

'Black families coming forward to adopt or foster see it as "helping" a child – in the West Indies, people help each other and the family may care for the child on a very long-term basis and still see the need to maintain contact with the natural family. When black families talk about coming forward to foster and adopt to help a child, they are talking about helping the whole family through helping the child.'

The formal approach of agencies to access was sometimes confusing, sometimes criticised:

'The only meaning of the word "access" back home is a road! We use the term "visiting". With that word the boundaries are clearer to the child – visiting is associated with going back home afterwards.'

'As a black foster parent, I don't feel threatened by a child starting to go back to visit their black parent. I know I can communicate with the black mother, whereas a white person may have doubts – there is a

communication gap which I would not have.'

A number of families had initiated or increased contact between the child and his or her relatives – in three cases with fathers with whom the child had previously had no contact for many years. There was particular concern about birth parents who were mentally ill, because of the awareness of the high incidence of mental illness among Afro-Caribbean immigrants and anxiety that the attitudes of social work agencies, particularly regarding restriction of access, were compounding this:

'To me, a person having a mental illness is just a person not well. If I was caring for children of a mother who was mentally ill then I would feel confident of her coming round and having a chat with her children and I wouldn't feel in any way threatened. Perhaps it was the way I was brought up. In a small community we shared griefs, everything. If one person was not well then that house would be just surrounded by all the neighbours – people would try to see what they could do to help. And first there would be many people offering to take the children.'

e) *Concern for the birth family* influenced some families in their thinking about adoption: 'I would not want to deprive them of their child ... stand in their way'.

'We wanted to know that the social services department had really tried hard to help the mother first because we didn't want the mother to feel cheated. We wanted to meet her, chat to her and see what she was like.'

One family had been persuaded, prior to the placement, to consider adoption rather than fostering of Sara, age nine, because of what the social worker and the panel had perceived as being in Sara's best interests. However, a year after placement, the family felt it would be inappropriate to pursue adoption because Sara valued her monthly visits to her mother. A contested adoption might jeopardise this and the good relationship which had been set up between the foster mother and the birth mother.

Generally it was important to families that workers did not feel that their hesitation regarding adoption indicated a lack of commitment or a mercenary motivation.

White social workers' attitudes to the families

White social workers' attitudes to black families were sometimes seen as unhelpful. Families felt that they were not trusted and that certain aspects of their child-rearing practices and culture were criticised without full understanding. This feeling may have been heightened by a family's previous experience of institutional racism and the perception of social services departments as destructive to black families:

'Some black families are shy or not so well educated and they fear that a white worker will just talk down to them.'

'Even if a black foster parent had reached the same level of education as a white worker there is still that inbred hesitance towards white people which stems back to slavery.'

One foster mother felt angry at the way a social worker appeared not to trust her:

'From the beginning she questioned why I wanted to do fostering. She thought I was doing it for the money. I said to her, "Money does not come into this". So it was a bad start. I said to myself, "This woman doesn't trust me". When Dwayne was going away with his school I told her what it would cost and she phoned up the school to check and then sent the money direct to the school instead of to me.'

Stereotyping of black families as obsessed with religion, having over-high expectations with regard to education and being too strict had affected the relationship of a number of black families and white social workers.

Religion
Black families, in general, emphasise the importance of church-going, and felt undermined by white social workers who let the child know that they did not share this view:

'I find that a lot of people in this country, white people, don't believe in God. When these people say it's wrong to force a child to go to church or

to put Christianity to them, they have it all wrong. If you have a kid in your home and he says no way is he going to church, then he has no respect for you. A kid is supposed to follow your example and your footsteps which you lay down for him.'

'I can't think of any families in the village where I lived as a child in Barbados that did not send their children to church. Parents see religion as the basis for the moral fibre of the child. You have to let the child know that Sunday is a different day. Over here it's different. I've got personal experience of being rejected by white churches, so it's not surprising that what you see on a Sunday morning are vans collecting children from different point and taking them to Sunday School, even if the parents never go near the church. I see going to church as very much part of roots. Don't forget that going to church is a social affair – it gives you another extended family. To me, to see a family going to church every Sunday as something negative is sad.'

Education

Black families were aware that the value they placed on education was criticised by white social workers who feared that a child would be pressured. They felt that the social workers lacked insight into the historical and social reasons for this:

'We are not that far away from slavery. I was the first secondary-educated person in my family – my mother was educated to the age of fourteen, her mother was educated even less because she had time off to look after the children, and her mother was educated even less and her mother was a slave, so education is comparatively new. Education is the open door, the pathway to anything you achieve in the West Indies. Because here there has been a good education system for much longer than we have had, you take it for granted.'

Concern was expressed about the relatively poor educational achieve-ments of children of West Indian parents growing up here compared with black people educated in the West Indies. Racist attitudes have been encountered in schools and some families have sent their children to Afro-Caribbean Saturday schools or to a private school set up by the Seventh Day Adventist Church. All parents were keen for their children to work hard to reach their potential:

'I stressed that very much to my son. Firstly I feel, and I am talking from experience, that what a white child will get away with at school a black child will not, so they have to behave well. I also feel very strongly that a black child has got to have twice as much education to get the same job as the white person, so I have always reinforced that to my children.'

Discipline

With regard to strictness and use of corporal punishment, families again found there was potential for misunderstanding between themselves and white social workers:

'Smacking is acceptable in the West Indies. If you didn't get smacked there would definitely be something wrong with that family and even the child would sense that. I have had experience of this with Maxine. I am not a smacker by nature so I would talk to Maxine and explain things to her but eventually she pushed and she pushed and she pushed until one day I gave her two smacks on her bottom. That afternoon, one by one, the friends she was playing with came to the door to check with me, "Is it true that you smacked Maxine?" I heard Maxine say to some little girl, "See, I told you I get smacked!". I suddenly realised that she needed to be accepted by other children and she had gone outside literally bragging that she had been smacked. So now she was the same as the other children! Now that she is fourteen I feel it would be degrading to smack her and we have gone back to what I originally wanted to do, which was to discuss and explain things.'

'If a foster mother was to walk around with a leather belt around her neck, that would be symbolic. A belt, slipper, shoe, every West Indian family has got some symbol of corporal punishment – a belt would be hanging on the door. The times it would be used (I am not saying that there aren't some families who go over the top) was not necessarily very often, but it would be used as a threat.'

'I could imagine that if you took a child from residential care who had not been brought up with that background, that initially the child could feel quite frightened of what could happen, but a year later the belt would have assumed its rightful proportions in the child's mind.'

It was the experience of some black foster parents that their interaction with members of their extended family was seen as a limitation rather than valued and in particular the role of the grandmother in the Afro-Caribbean family structure was not always understood. Some families were bewildered by the bureaucratic response to children spending weekends or short holidays with relatives or friends.

Financial aspects
The need for financial support has been on occasion a source of friction between social workers and families. Project social workers had gained the impression that the income of the black families seen was somewhat lower than that of the white families, and this assumption was tested by comparing the incomes, as stated at the time of acceptance, of the 42 families with whom children were placed between April 1984 and March 1986. In fact, it was found that there was little difference between the average income of the black and white groups and the distribution was similar.

In the lowest income group, the black families comprised three single parents (of twelve families). The white group included two single parents and three unemployed heads of household (of 29 families). However, black families were slightly under-represented in the two higher income groups (£15,000 to £20,000 per annum and £20,000 plus per annum).

There were significantly more black families in which both parents were in full employment (seven out of the twelve black families compared with six of the 29 white families). Only two black women were described as 'housewives' whereas twelve white women were. Thus, in a higher proportion of black families, both parents continued to work after placement, which was possible in part because of the support of the extended family and in part because in most families, older children were being placed.

The difficulties arising about financial assistance were mainly in the area of discretionary payments, particularly for clothing and holidays. Families felt that it was more expensive to maintain the Afro-Caribbean culture in this country. For example, skin and hair products are generally more costly, as are ingredients for Afro-Caribbean dishes. Food was seen as an integral part of people's identity and as a way of maintaining the culture. Visits to the West Indies were seen as valuable, but generally families needed assistance from the social services department towards the child's expenses:

'Visiting the West Indies – that's where their roots are, so that's extremely important. In this country, they always refer to our children as children of immigrants so therefore it is important they they visit their mother's country or parents' country.'

'As you know, we took Carl back home with us. The social worker got the fares paid for us but it did not cover his keep. Right away you are talking about a suitcase of clothes because you have to change them every day. So clearly, it costs a lot for clothing and where we live in the country you find that travelling around costs a lot of money as well.'

Regular churchgoing meant that often the clothes that the children came with were unsuitable and families did not always find initial clothing grants readily obtainable:

'I couldn't be going out and having a child with me that looked scruffy. What are people going to say? They are going to say it's because it's not his kid. People don't realise that you don't get the help to buy the clothes. So I make sure that what I have I spend on them because I'd be ashamed.'

Families frequently felt it was humiliating to ask for financial assistance yet they could not manage without. The frustration felt about financial difficulties may have been compounded because of the families' sense of being misunderstood and mistrusted.

The adjustment of children and teenagers to living in a black family
In addition to coming to terms with their identity, a number of the children placed, particularly the teenagers, found expectations of their foster families contrasted sharply with that of residential workers. Black parents felt it necessary to be strict in order to help the child understand the importance of respect in the Afro-Caribbean family and also because they had experience of some police officers and some teachers picking on the black child:

'When they came here, they had a rotten attitude. In the home they don't have anyone to provide them with guidance. When they feel like *going to bed they go to bed, and if they feel like watching television they stay down and watch television. I think the attitude in the home is not good enough – there are so many different people dealing with them, sometimes a kid will refuse to do what he has been asked to do and nothing is done about it.'*

'If anyone came from Barnardo's or any local authority they would be proud to see how the boys are now. Dwayne has more manners now than he had and whereas before they came I was worried that they might do something unfit, now I can guarantee that they won't, because I took them and I showed them first to know how to respect people.'

'Marvin was allowed and took it for granted, that he could talk back to people who were his caretakers. That was not tolerated in my house. That was unacceptable behaviour so it was quite a big adjustment for him and quite difficult for us.'

Sometimes the way in which social workers attempted to help teenagers who were having difficulty adjusting was seen as threatening because it undermined the authority of the parent: for example, a social worker gave a child permission to attend a youth club without consulting the foster parent (who would not have allowed it); another social worker made important decisions regarding the child during a telephone conversation with her, and the foster parent learned of the decision from the child; and a senior social worker at a review suggested to a thirteen year old that the foster family's expectations were 'too high'. The boy interpreted this as 'unreasonably high' and his behaviour subsequently deteriorated. During recent years, children and young people in care have increasingly participated in case conferences and reviews, but a style of working which involves the child but excludes the parent is alien to many black families:

'With a child with behavioural problems I feel that the less he sees of a lot of very important people the better for him, because when he sees all these people he thinks he is over-important and this affects him. When Marvin attended a review with senior social workers and all those, he used to get really high. He would play off one against the other so I needed to trust the social worker and I needed to know that the social worker trusted me.'

Effective means of offering support

The two most urgent needs for black children in care were identified as:

– the opportunity of contact with black people before being placed – 'not just black people in the kitchen or who clean the floor'

– and for social workers to have an awareness of the history, culture and experiences of black people, particularly the impact of racism.

One foster parent expressed the view that there should be more black social workers, 'preferably black West Indian social workers, not Afro-Caribbean offspring'. She felt that black workers brought up in this country did not always have the same levels of awareness and understanding as social workers raised in the West Indies. Families did not say that white workers could *not* offer effective post-placement support: some had had very helpful links with white workers:

'*I found the white workers very supportive. I don't think you can just appoint black workers and leave them to get on with it. They should work alongside white workers so that knowledge and skill can be shared and developed. It is most important for white workers to learn about black history, to acknowledge racism. It is also important for black workers and white workers to acknowledge their prejudices.*'

There was also a plea, in part to do with unease about authority, for less 'bureaucracy', for reviews not to require a written contribution from the foster parent unless they wished to offer one; for senior personnel attending reviews to be sensitive as to how the child viewed their presence; and for more willingness to trust the foster parents' judgement.

'*Marvin was in my hands and I feel very strongly that if he was in my home I should raise him the way I wanted to raise him. Because I had a lot of interviews before he was placed with me and therefore they must have trusted me so therefore I wanted to be left alone.*'

It was seen as helpful to be able to telephone or speak to someone for support who had 'no powers' – another foster parent, or a worker in a voluntary agency.

'*The fantasy I had was that if I was to ring the social worker when I was upset that might all be written down and a meeting would be called! Somewhere impartial is needed.'*

The value of the preparation groups attended during the assessment was stressed:

'I got a lot of things out of the preparation group that came up, sometimes years later, which I was able to recognise. So when things did happen I did not feel so isolated.'

A number of families also found the regular adoptive and foster parent groups – a combination of social events and discussion evenings – a useful means of offering and receiving support as well as an opportunity for mutual sharing with project social workers. In addition, links could be made with other families.

A more flexible and generous approach to adoption allowances could perhaps lead to a few more black children being adopted by black parents.

The fact that so many of the children placed have become well integrated into their new families and have grown in self-esteem and confidence about their own identity reflects well on the commitment and care of the families who have helped them make this difficult adjustment.

Postscript
We have seen a change in the last six months in the pattern of families contacting the project and recently have had a number of young Anglo-Afro-Caribbean or Afro-Caribbean families, born or brought up in the UK, applying to adopt pre-school children. All the parents who contributed to this chapter had come to the UK from the West Indies as young adults so the chapter does not reflect what may be a somewhat different perspective among the generation of Afro-Caribbean people born here.

With acknowledgement to Pearl, Beryl, Rosemary, Bertram, Beryl, Jean and Lorretta and to colleagues in the Homefinding Project: Mike Allen, Helen Caine, Ann Haigh, Beverlin McKenzie, Marie Ramdhan and Pauline Wellington

5 Specialist ventures in post-adoption services

Included in this chapter are accounts of projects which are contributing something new or special to post-adoption services. All of them offer a service to birth parents, adopted people and adopters. There are surely other projects and schemes which could have been included but which we do not know about: in the meantime, these examples of contemporary developments will, we hope, inspire more post-adoption support work.

THE POST-ADOPTION CENTRE
Phillida Sawbridge

In August 1986 a new centre came into being in London, offering services to any of the participants in an adoption. Adoptive parents, adopted people, brothers, sisters, and other relatives of adopted people, and parents who have relinquished a child for adoption are all invited to use the centre. We are particularly conscious of the hitherto unmet needs of multi-racial families, black adopters, and in particular black birth parents who carry the additional burden of political and cultural pressures. On offer are not only advice, counselling and information, meetings with others to work out concerns in a group, and seminars or public meetings on relevant topics, but also the opportunity for involvement in producing educational materials on adoption.

The thinking behind such a centre had been developing over a long period, but several factors had a major influence on the direction that thinking took. The evidence of the need for post-adoption services had been growing, from the avid response to earlier initiatives such as the adoptive parents' discussion groups run by the Guild of Service in Edinburgh in the 1960s and the London Borough of Hounslow in the 1970s, to the very clear indications of what parents of 'special needs' children wanted, as revealed by Catherine Macaskill's study of the 'Parents for Children' agency's placements in 1985 (summarised in

Adoption & Fostering 9 1 1985 and 9 2 1985).

Adoptive parents had also been making their needs increasingly felt through their own organisation, PPIAS (Parent-to-Parent Information on Adoption Services: see below). Mutual support and advice meet many of these needs, but members have also stated a desire for professional services where adoption is better understood. Adopted people have set up their own self-help organisation, NORCAP (National Organisation for the Counselling of Adoptees and their Parents: see also below) and, while they give support to any of the participants in an adoption, they too have welcomed having a place to which they can refer people who may need more than their own group can offer.

People who have always been neglected are the birth parents of adopted children. Although adoption agencies may have told them to come back if they want further service, few do go back. Many never worked with an agency, and in any case a large number of voluntary agencies have closed down in the last decade. Meanwhile, the 1975 Children Act gave adopted people from the age of 18 in England and Wales the right of access to their original birth records and made it very much easier for them to trace their birth parents. Many people have welcomed the thought of being traced by the child they relinquished years before, but some have never told a soul about that child and dread the disruption to their lives of being 'found'. Either way, there have been no specific professional services to which they were invited to turn for advice, or anywhere they could meet others who had had the same experience. None of the women who attended the first group at the centre for birth mothers had ever met someone else who acknowledged parting with a child for adoption.

Adopted people wanting access to their birth records are required, if adopted before 1975, to be counselled by a designated person beforehand. Many of the counsellors are local authority social workers who for the first time are meeting numbers of adopted people and learning how they view their adoptions. This has produced still more evidence of the need for long-term services to be available to adoptive families. Telling adopted children about their status and origins and responding to their interest in finding out more about their parentage can be a tense and difficult matter for some adoptive parents, who welcome help in resolving the dilemmas which their children face in terms of divided loyalties and their wish to protect all parties while satisfying their own need for information.

Statutory counselling has provided some of this help, but it may not always come at the right time. Younger people may need it, or those who have long since gained access to their records and who are struggling with the final stages of a 'search' for a birth relative. Also, very many people never receive formal counselling because they know their name of origin and are able to apply for their birth certificate directly. We are finding that many adult adopted people are asking the centre to act as an intermediary at the point of contacting a birth parent. Both parties may need intensive counselling and support over a certain period, and this is time-consuming work which statutory departments may be ill-equipped to do.

For all the groups of people involved, a neutral and informed service can fill a real gap. The majority of adoptive families function in a perfectly satisfactory way, with open communication, trust and mutual concern, and will not want any outside help. But families created by adoption have specific attributes which other families have not and, as some of those attributes may involve mystery, mourning and doubt, it is reasonable to think of making support available for those who are affected.

There is a strong argument for support services to be offered by the placing agencies, so that the body which acted as intermediary in the bringing together of parents and child can continue to support the family thus created. Where there is long-term continuity of staff in the agency, and the pre-placement process has been designed to establish trust and a positive working relationship between agency and adopters, this makes sense. Where, however, adopters feel there is no one they know in the agency within six months or a year of taking their child, or where they have felt so scrutinised and exposed by the process of approval that they are glad to close the door on the agency, then it is unlikely they will return for support. It is hard for adopters to acknowledge doubts or difficulties as parents. They have had to go through a process of approval no other parents have to, and if they were infertile they are often secretly very unsure of their right to a child at all. If things go wrong, or they feel challenged or threatened in their role as parents, it is hard for them to find the courage to expose what they may see as failure. It therefore seemed that an independent centre for adoption counselling would meet a need.

The intention behind the setting-up of the centre was to offer a professional service free of any direct links with specific agencies. The blueprint called for comfortable attractive surroundings where people could feel at ease and where, as far as possible, adoption was not seen as something necessarily bringing 'problems' but rather as a form of family-creation differing from others and therefore deserving a place of its own in which thoughts and ideas could be aired. For instance, the very first public seminar looked at 'Eleven years of access to birth-records' – a topic of common interest to everyone concerned with adoption. People are invited to come and browse through the books, journals and articles on display and to contribute to video films, to be used in public education as well as in discussion groups for other participants. Workshops have been mounted to help parents tackle questions like: how do you explain to pre-school age children about adoption, their own or someone else's, and what it may or may not be appropriate to say to other people? Adoptive parents pool their views and experiences together with those of the professional workers who run the groups. The workshops aim to help people better understand the reasons for certain behaviour, or what children of different ages can be expected to comprehend. Participants glean ideas for using stories, play and other techniques. There is thus one place where experience and expertise is being built up, which can be fed back to people involved in adoption outside.

The centre is also keen to become a place in which people can try out other forms of therapy which do not necessarily involve talking. Some families, for instance, have children who were scarred by early deprivation, separations or ill-treatment. The parents have tried all kinds of 'talking therapies' and still feel they are not getting through to their child. At the centre it is possible to try out various techniques to help free children's feelings. Play and drama therapy, art therapy, therapeutic holding and 'sculpting' are examples of approaches which have either already been tried, or could be available. Some parents are at their wits' end trying to understand and deal with violent or rejecting adolescents, and the centre is keen to explore or develop ways of helping such families. For a minority of enquirers, a professional psychiatric service may be needed, and the centre has developed a variety of links with therapeutic services. Through the Consultant Psychiatrist in the Children's Department of the Maudsley Hospital, the centre has access to a wide range of services including assessment, individual or family therapy, and behaviour therapy. The centre's staff have regular consultations with two psychiatrists and a family therapist.

The centre is also trying to develop links with social workers, psychologists, psychiatrists and other professionals elsewhere, both in order to establish appropriate points of referral if necessary, and also to try to improve services generally by passing on what is being learnt at the centre. The work is being monitored through a university department, statistics are being collected, and it is planned to publish reports which will analyse the range of concerns people bring and discuss reponses to them. This is all part of an attempt to ensure that whatever is learned at the centre about adoption practice and the needs of participants can be disseminated as widely as possible, so that the institution of adoption itself can be better understood. Other approaches include offering seminars and workshops and, perhaps in the future, inviting agencies and social services departments to second staff to work in the centre and thus gain first-hand experience.

There may prove to be many shortcomings in the way the centre has been devised. The telephone counselling service could easily be swamped. The demand for individual interviews and for group-work could be far greater than the resources permit, and hopes may be raised which cannot be fulfilled. There are also valid arguments against providing a separate service for adoptive families. Don't other families have similar worries and concerns, and shouldn't all the helping professions be geared to working with family problems, adolescent difficulties and poor communication? Isn't it over-emphasising the difference to offer adoptive families a separate service? Yet the reasoning behind the centre still stands. The differences are there and, for too long, adoptive families have had to stifle their acknowledgement of them. A greater social openness and changing views about family relationships, illegitimacy, infertility and child-rearing have also affected adoption. It is to be hoped that in the long term, all agencies will prepare adoptive parents and work with birth parents in such a way that a continuing service will seem a natural part of the process for those who need it: a service which could ideally be offered both by the placing agencies and by independent specialist centres like the Post-Adoption Centre.

THE NATIONAL ORGANISATION FOR THE COUNSELLING OF ADOPTEES AND THEIR PARENTS (NORCAP)
Pam Hodgkins

NORCAP was set up with the primary intention of offering practical advice to those adult adopted people who wished to renew contact with birth relatives. It very soon became clear that practical advice was not enough; adopted people, birth parents and adoptive parents all wanted *someone to talk to*. Today, all the services NORCAP offers reflect the need of those involved in adoption to be able to talk freely and at length to someone who understands. Whilst we, as volunteers, acknowledge and frequently need the help and support of professional adoption workers, we find that the people who come to us often do so because we are not professional or 'official'.

Adoption workers can be seen by their clients to be all-powerful and post-adoption work is still a new area. For many of our members, the adoption officer has become 'the person who took my baby away'! Rarely, if ever, true, but an interpretation of past events that enables the birth mother to cope with her experience and actions. For adoptive parents the social worker was someone to impress, who could veto or support the application to adopt, who seemed to control the supply of the desired commodity. The need to convince the agency that they are good parents, and perhaps the agency's need to be reassured that their judgement was correct, are not conducive to recognising and remedying later problems. Adopted people, too, see the agency as all-powerful – the institution that determined the nature of their lives. The authority which may know more about them than they know themselves, having the power to give or to withhold, without reason, information which may open closed doors. Few birth records applicants – persons of 18 or over wishing to trace their origins – expect to find the agency friendly, open and supportive; many are pleasantly surprised, but the invisible barrier between the one who knows and the one who has to ask is seldom completely removed.

Not surprisingly, therefore, many people wish to move away from everything official and seek advice, support or a listening ear from someone they anticipate will understand. The understanding is assumed because the helper is known to have personal experience of the situation. In reality none of us has a monopoly of experience but at NORCAP we can say that everyone who answers a call on behalf of the organisation has some personal involvement with adoption. Is a 35-year-old adopted person, whose attempt to renew contact with her birth mother has been rejected, really able to offer a better service to a woman of the same age desperate to hear from the son she placed for adoption 17 years earlier, than a qualified and experienced counsellor? Perhaps the answer should be 'no', but the expectation of the mother is that understanding and help will be forthcoming from the volunteer, whilst the professional worker, she imagines, will be judgmental and patronising. The poor professional has a great deal of work to do before ever reaching the starting line.

Having admitted that we have a certain advantage, can NORCAP measure up to the expectations? We can only try. All we have to offer is ouselves, our willingness to share our experiences and what we have learned from those experiences. Individually that may not be very much but collectively it represents a body of expertise. People come to us because we are amateurs but they expect us to respond as experts. This is a contradiction we have tried to overcome by yet another contradiction – training our volunteers to act professionally, not through a potted professional course but through opportunities to look objectively at situations they may face. Our volunteers meet together to consider rights and obligations regarding confidentiality, personal involvement, taking initiatives and assisting members to reach the solution that suits the needs of the member rather than the needs of the volunteer. Owning up to our limitations and prejudices is a vital part of the learning process.

Our trained volunteers are expected to answer practical questions about legislation and queries involving the searching process. They also listen for the deeper personal questions that are not being asked. They do not claim they can always help, but they should know where help can be obtained. They expect their credibility to be checked out by a simple factual question, knowing that the real reason for the call will come after the, 'oh, just before I go could you tell me . . .' We find adopted people will test out questions on someone else's mum before risking hurting their own. And they are more likely to be 30 and curious than 20 and desperate.

A small group of volunteers has attended seminars and explored various means of operating an intermediary service – that is, a service to enable adopted people, birth parents and adoptive parents to meet. This is an onerous task for a volunteer but one that a voluntary group is uniquely qualified to undertake. We write on notelets from our home address, for that is where we work. We can genuinely write on behalf of 'our friend' for our members are not clients and are encouraged to choose an intermediary they feel 'in tune' with. When the birth parent who has been approached rings the intermediary one evening, as requested, she does not first have to brave a receptionist, clerk and secretary, as our own families are warned to let us answer the phone whenever we are expecting a 'special call'. We can expand on the vague notelet telling the caller how much we have in common with our friend: children, hobbies, age and that we are both adopted. 'Ah yes', says the caller and the jigsaw begins to be pieced together. NORCAP intermediaries do not act for any one party; they are responsible for cultivating the initial growth of a new relationship.

NORCAP sees its role as drawing our members back down to earth when they are as high as a kite, and picking them up when they find themselves in a deep dark hole. We listen, we comment, we are an 'advice group' on many people's lists of advice groups, but we try not to advise. Having identified what people need us to do, we try to respond. Recognising individual needs has shown us patterns and trends, flaws in existing services and areas where new services need to be developed. We either try to meet these needs ourselves or we encourage (and/or plead with) the official side of post-adoption services to respond appropriately.

THE TRIANGLE GROUP
Margaret and Mervyn Humphreys

Aims and origins
We established the Triangle Group in Nottingham in December, 1984, as a small-scale, voluntary project, designed to extend the rather limited range of support systems available to adult adopted people, birth and adoptive parents. As well as providing a local contribution to the development of an adequate network of support facilities for the adults in the adoption triangle, we wanted to test the relevance of recent American developments, in adoption research and practice, in an English context.[1] In particular, we were keen to explore the potential of groupwork as a means of tackling the dilemmas and difficulties faced by the different members of the triangle.

Following the example set by the Post-adoption Centre for Education and Research in Palo Alto, California, we decided to work with a mixed group of adult adopted people and birth and adoptive parents towards two related goals. First, we hoped that the different perspectives represented by all sides of the adoption triangle would help members who needed to reflect on, and reconsider, their particular experience of adoption. Second, major issues – such as the impact of loss and separation on personality development and identity formation – could be discussed and, we hoped, either resolved or managed in a more satisfactory way.

Although we are employed as social workers in a social services department, we have established our project as a voluntary initiative, in our spare time, for several reasons. Just as the traditional recruitment methods of certain adoption agencies have often failed to attract the interest of black families, so various cultural factors or myths associated with social services departments may reduce the flow of referrals to such departments from members of the adoption triangle. Among these psychological obstacles we would include the battered public image of local authority social workers, their association with stigmatised sections of the community, and their department's status as an adoption agency.[2] Also, people in need of a flexible, rapid and personal response might not regard themselves as a priority for a large organisation coping with a heavy workload and multiple statutory duties. Finally, we felt that, if we operated within the statutory agency, it might be assumed that we had access to confidential information about group members which could introduce an awkward, 'power' dimension into our relationships with the group. We wanted to remove this possibility and to work with our membership on a more equal footing. We felt that this was crucial to the development of trusting relationships with those adopted adults who had not been informed of their adoptive status during their childhood or adolescence.

Although we lack certain resources available to statutory workers, our voluntary position has enabled us to avoid some of their dilemmas. Unlike birth records counsellors, for example, we do not need to reflect on the implications of compulsory counselling or the merits of an open or closed policy on files.[3] We do not have any compulsory powers or duties in relation to the group members, we do not maintain any personal files and the only information we possess about the members is what they share with us.

Organisational links and liaison

As some aspects of this venture threatened to lead us into uncharted waters and as we lacked a reference group of colleagues employing similar methods, we chose various organisations as an anchor point for the group. We asked the self-help team in Nottingham to include details of the Triangle Group in its local directory of groupwork resources and to give us access to other channels of communication. As a result we were invited to submit a short article to our local evening newspaper, which now also publishes a list of our meetings on a monthly basis. The self-help team has arranged a telephone answering service for us and has provided a room near the city centre for our meetings. This has helped to reinforce our status as an independent, voluntary initiative. Members of the adoption triangle therefore have a choice between turning to an adoption agency – which might perhaps have been concerned with their placement – or seeking an alternative, neutral source of advice.

Before our first meeting we had developed close links with the National Organisation for Counselling Adoptees and their Parents (NORCAP) which provided financial support, further publicity through a newsletter and sound guidance and advice. For professional consultation on legal and social work issues we used local colleagues who acted as a critical and appreciative audience while we expressed our doubts, dilemmas and designs for future activities.

We were encouraged by the helpful reactions of local voluntary adoption agencies and grateful for the co-operation of Nottinghamshire Social Services Department in providing birth records counsellors with details of the group and the procedures for referring potential members.

Several local organisations agreed to display our posters giving details of the group's aims and membership, but we did not launch a major publicity campaign as we did not want to offer a diluted level of support to a large number of people. We preferred to offer a more concentrated service of a group meeting lasting at least two-and-a-half hours every fortnight. In addition we answered telephone enquiries from a variety of referral agents and potential members. As these activities were conducted outside, and in addition to, our full-time employment, we needed to set limits on our time and energy to avoid the dangers of overloading and exhaustion.

The group members

We have generally worked with a membership of eight individuals, with a futher six members having a more marginal involvement. Some adopted people have attended every meeting for three or four months and then left the group after having experienced a positive reunion with their birth parents. Others have attended regularly for over a year, and a small group have attended less regularly.

The members vary enormously in background and employment, and their ages range from 25 to 60. Most of them are married and are parents and there are roughly equal numbers of men and women.

Two thirds are adopted people, and almost one third are birth parents. There has not been more than a token level of representation from adoptive parents. Although we have received many telephone enquiries from adopters, these have rarely resulted in later attendance at group meetings. Perhaps this is not the kind of post-adoption service adoptive parents want or need. But many adopted people need support before they can face their adoptive parents with their intention to seek information about their origins, or their success in tracing members of their original family. Several of our members had waited until their adoptive parents were dead before making sustained efforts to trace their birth parents; few had adoptive parents who knew of their intention to search. Consequently, many meetings consisted of members representing only two sides of the adoption triangle. However, we tried to ensure that the perspectives and possible reactions of adoptive parents were included as an important element in our discussions.

Motivations and outcomes

The majority of members decided to attend for two related reasons. Many wanted practical advice about the mechanics of tracing relatives and obtaining background information about original families, and most were seeking an opportunity to reflect on their experience of adoption and the different stages and decisions involved in tracing. For example, the ethics of different methods of tracing and the possible repercussions for themselves, their partners and children, as well as the potential impact on those they wished to find, were all significant issues, which concerned birth parents as much as adopted people.

Much attention was devoted to the need for adequate preparation for the different members of the group at various stages. For example, potential members were interviewed before they joined the group to explain the nature of its aims, membership and activities, and to assess whether their particular needs could be met by the group. In some instances, further individual sessions were necessary before new members felt sufficient confidence to attend and share their very private concerns in a group context.

Many of the adopted people who joined the group had not been provided with an early and adequate account of their origins and the circumstances surrounding their placement with their adoptive parents. Some had not been told of their adoptive status at all but had discovered it for themselves during their adult years, or had been given false information which had served to discredit the character and motives of their birth parents. We received enquiries, too, from some people who believed that they were adopted, as they had not been cared for by their parents and their original surname had been changed; but later research showed that they were not the subject of an adoption order. All the members who had been given misleading accounts of their biological roots or of the reasons for their adoption felt a compelling need to discover the facts about their parents and their placement.

All our members in this position have needed considerable support in coming to understand the nature of the fears and anxieties which led their adoptive parents to deceive them about these critical issues. Many have found it helpful and illuminating to compare and contrast their accounts of their birth parents with the actual experiences of those birth parents attending the group. This interchange often enables adopted people to assess the accuracy of different parts of their story. Similarly, those who have traced their birth parents can question the birth parent members about the short- and long-term consequences of reunions, or about the least disruptive methods of making the initial contact. Again, the presence of a birth father in the group has helped to widen the horizons of those adopted members whose focus of attention and concern becomes fixated on their birth mother.

Although most of the birth parents and adopted people attending the group were married and enjoyed a variety of social relationships, many felt that their family and friends lacked a depth of understanding about the emotional implications of their experience of adoption. They therefore valued their membership of the group as it provided an opportunity to share their experiences in a safe and accepting environment and, in the words of one birth parent, 'a release from the internal prison of guilt'.

For many birth parents, the group meetings were used to reflect on the pain and loss which they continued to feel after being separated from their children for over 25 years. All retained vivid and detailed memories of the events surrounding the placement of their children but few had been given, or had felt able to accept, earlier opportunities for discussion. Several birth-parent members sought reassurance from adopted people about the quality of life and relationships within adoptive families.

Much of the work within the group could be seen as a preparation for coping with the positive and negative outcomes of anticipated and actual reunions. Our experience of reunions suggests that the inevitable cross-currents of powerful feelings place particular stress and responsibility on the adopted person initiating the meeting. It is frequently their ability to anticipate and contain their own and others' anxieties and doubts which determines the outcome of the reunion. The professional group leader must therefore ensure that sufficient ego-building work has been undertaken with those who are about to meet their birth parents. Other crucial ingredients for successful reunions include a clarification of motives and expectations, and an assessment of the strengths and weaknesses of those directly involved in the reunion and of their social networks.

We have been encouraged by the positive results produced by this mixture of professional intervention and self-help resources within the group. The majority have achieved their goals of meeting members of their original family. We do not yet have a sufficiently large sample of reunions which have lasted more than a year to be able to make judgements about the long-term impact on those concerned. Wherever possible, we have worked with all the members of a specific adoption triangle and combined individual work involving adopted people, for example, with sessions involving both them and their birth mothers – and, if at all possible, their adoptive parents.

Attendance at group meetings has continued during and after reunions. Some members have traced birth parents shortly before or after a birth parent has died, and have used the group to help cope with their grief. Others have achieved seemingly impossible goals by meeting birth parents who live abroad, or tracing relatives within a few months of joining the group after spending several years engaged in fruitless searching. Many members report less dramatic but equally significant results such as coming to terms with feelings of guilt, or a poor self-image, as well as improving their confidence and ability to assert themselves in social and family situations.

Those members who have traced and met their birth parents now have a more accurate and comprehensive understanding of their early life history. As well as gaining a more complete picture of the crucial events and significant individuals of their infancy, many adopted members have also been able to help their birth parents come to terms with *their* feelings of guilt. In addition, some have also found themselves in the unusual position of providing their adoptive parents with new information about their placement which was not made available by the agency involved. In order to preserve vital details and documents, we have advised and encouraged such adopted members to compile their own version of their life story, or birth family album, using correspondence relating to their search as well as photographs of their birth parents and their original birth certificate.

Conclusion

After three years work in this complex area of post-adoption support, we remain convinced of the value of skilled intervention based on a view of adoption as a dynamic process with far-reaching emotional implications for all the members of the triangle. We are also more aware of the limitations of approaches which focus on one member of the triangle or one stage in the adoption process. Through the Triangle Group we have tried to combine therapeutic and self-help strategies to design a project which merits further consideration by those concerned with post-adoption services.

References

1 Sorosky A D, Baran A and Pannor R *The adoption triangle* Doubleday, 1984.

2 Golding P and Middleton S *Images of Welfare* Basil Blackwell, 1982.

3 Haimes E and Timms N *Adoption, identity and social policy* Gower, 1985.

PARENT TO PARENT INFORMATION ON ADOPTION SERVICES
Philly Morrall

Parent to Parent Information on Adoption Services (PPIAS) was formed in 1971 by a group of parents who had adopted children then considered 'hard to place' and who had had great difficulty in finding out which voluntary and local authority adoption agencies were in a position to organise this kind of adoption. The group aims to help other potential adopters by passing on information about how and where to apply, and to provide support, advice and encouragement for prospective and existing adopters, and for long-term foster parents.

PPIAS hopes that a better network of information will help many more people to adopt children who would otherwise grow up in care. There are now over 100 local contacts all over the country, who collect as much information as they can about the agencies in their own area. All share their knowledge with new members. Most co-ordinators hold meetings where a wide variety of topics related to adoption can be discussed.

For prospective and existing adopters, sharing experiences with other adopters can be very helpful and encouraging at any stage of adoption. Some aspects of adoption which families have found it valuable to discuss are:
– talking about adoption with their children
– explaining and understanding children's past experiences
– getting advice on legal complexities
– suggesting ways of coping with behavioural difficulties
– arranging respite care for handicapped children
– gaining help in seeking professional advice
– having the opportunity to 'let off steam' with others who will understand
– sharing the experience of becoming a racially mixed family.

Adopted children, too, often appreciate contact with other children who are also adopted. PPIAS branches usually hold some family events such as summer picnics, Christmas parties, etc, where children can meet other adopted children. From a child's point of view it's very comforting to have some friends who are adopted. It makes the whole thing seem more normal and less 'different', and it gives children the opportunity to share similar feelings and experiences. They enjoy going to the picnics and meeting their friends. Knowing other adoptive families with new children and babies arriving keeps the subject near the surface and discussable.

PPIAS now has a wide membership of adoptive families with very varied and valuable experiences of adoption. Within the group there are those with experience of adoption of tiny healthy infants through to teenagers and handicapped children, of all ages and of many different racial origins.

PPIAS can put families in touch with one another for their mutual support in both joys and difficulties. It acts as an information exchange, and has produced an extensive booklist and a resource pack for mixed-race families as well as leaflets on aspects of adoption. In addition it publishes an informative newsletter three times a year.

6 Adoption and therapy

There is increasing co-operation between adoption workers, child psychiatrists, child guidance clinics and therapists. A new interest in each other's work is growing and we are learning what we can do separately and what we can do together, to offer the best post-adoption service. The contributors to this chapter do not speak for their professions, but from their own experiences. They may have differing views of adoption and of therapy, but each one of them is working closely with adoptive families and with adoption agencies. Other clinics and psychiatrists are, no doubt, also concerned with adoption, and this chapter does not claim to be a comprehensive view of psychiatric services to adopted people.

POST-ADOPTION WORK BY THE CHILD PSYCHIATRIST
Stephen Wolkind

To some extent, child psychiatric clinics have for many years been offering a post-adoption service. This has not been planned and in many units workers have probably not even been aware that this is the case. However, data from both sides of the Atlantic consistently indicate that, by comparison with their numbers in the general population, adopted children and their families are constantly over-represented in clinic referrals. For many families this proves to be the most appropriate way of dealing with difficulties with their adopted child. Unfortunately, in other cases the results of referral are less satisfactory, perhaps because of problems specific to adoption that may be perplexing to those who have limited experience of the process. If the psychiatrist is suspicious of adoption and of adopting parents, this attitude can communicate itself to a family. One parent described to me in extreme terms how, after telling a child psychiatrist of the many problems they were having with their son, received as the only answer an astonished 'But why then don't you send him back?'. Even if this level of response is not typical, the problems presented by some adopted children can be puzzling for the psychiatrist. In particular, the sometimes bizarre behaviours and lack of emotional responsiveness shown by previously abused children, even years after adoption, can frustrate the child psychiatrist in his or her efforts to offer constructive help.

Because of my links with several adoption agencies, I probably see more families in my practice than does the average child psychiatrist. In this chapter I shall first explore why adopted children are referred more than others and then give a description of the most common types of problems which I see in my clinics.

Adopted children: referral to child psychiatrists

The first major contribution to discussion about this topic was that of Schechter,[1] who was struck by the very large number of adopted children being seen in child psychiatric units in South California. In virtually all of them a disproportionate number had been referred; in his own clinic there were over ten times as many as would have been expected. A series of similar findings, though perhaps not as extreme, were reported from other centres. In Britain, Humphrey and Ounstead[2] reported that in Oxfordshire three per cent of children seen in clinics were adopted. Their percentage in the population was under half that figure. High proportions, too, were described in residential units for disturbed or delinquent children.[3]

There are a number of points to be made about these statistics. First, they were collected during the 1960s. Most of the children would have been adopted by their new families during the 1950s, a time when it was unusual to place older children or those with special needs in families. It is therefore possible that current clinic figures would be even higher.[4] Second, though they show that adopted children are more likely than others to see a child psychiatrist, the figures also demonstrate that the *majority* of adopted children are not in fact referred to clinics. The third point is that though they show a higher than expected referral rate, this does not necessarily mean that adopted children are actually more likely to be disturbed than others. It is possible that the excessive referrals predominantly reflect the concerns and attitudes of professionals, rather than the true rate of disturbance amongst these children. There is indeed some evidence that professionals do react differently to adopted children than they might do to others.[5]

To answer this latter point we need to turn to total population studies. In Britain important information has been obtained from the National Child Development Study, a long-term follow up of a group of children born in 1958.[6] At aged seven, adopted boys showed slightly higher rates of disturbance than other boys, but girls showed no excess of disorders. By age eleven, both boys and girls showed significantly increased rates of psychological difficulties. It is thus probable that the high rate of referral is a result both of professional attitudes and of a truly higher rate of disorder amongst the children. Lest this statement cause concern as to whether adoption is necessarily the best course of action for certain children, it is necessary to add at this point that the rates of disorder in adopted children, though higher than average, are very much lower than those found amongst children in other anomalous situations, such as foster or residential care, or indeed amongst those living with their biological parents in disharmonious families.[7] In addition it is reassuring to note that those studies which have looked at adult adoptees find the majority do perfectly well.[8]

Clinical experience

Before describing the types of clinical problems seen, it is worth contrasting the handling, in a child psychiatric clinic, of adopted children with those who are fostered. With a foster child there is always the lingering thought that if things really are too bad, advice can be given to the social worker that it would be better to end the placement. With the adopted child, despite the misunderstanding of a few clinicians, there is no way out, and the family and therapist *have* to find a solution. These differing attitudes of professionals, combined with the greater autonomy of the adopted family, predict that the outcome of intervention by clinics should be much better in adoptive than in foster families.

That this is the case is certainly my clinical impression, even though there are no hard data to confirm this.

Post-adoption syndromes

Early psychiatric writings about adoption often attempted to demon-strate that specific types of disorders were seen in adoptive children. It was, for example, felt that a picture of uncontrolled aggression was characteristic of the disturbed adopted child. More systematic study demonstrated clearly that this was not the case. More popular, and with more basis to it, was the notion of the adolescent identity crisis, though even this, as I shall suggest below, appears to be a far less substantial concept than was first thought. What does seem to be the case, however, with current types of adoption, is that we are seeing unusual clinical pictures which do not fit easily into any known psychiatric syndrome. These occur in children who have been chronically neglected, often abused, and may have had numerous changes of placement prior to their adoption. There appear to be two components to the picture. The first is an emotional blunting. The child shows no extremes of emotion. He or she will learn to laugh because the rest of the family is doing so, but there seems to be no depth of happiness or joy behind the laughter. Tears are rarely, if ever, seen. There can be a strange compliance with adults' demands, and parents can be embarrassed trying to describe this. One family demanded an urgent appointment and apologetically stated when they arrived, 'David is too good, anything you ask him to do he will do without question'. Behind this awkward description of a problem which, they realised, many parents might see as a major asset, was a real distress that something was missing in David. The second component is an odd inability to grasp the basic rules of family life. Parents can speak with great puzzlement of the fact that, even after years in their family, their child still does not appear to realise that lunch always follows breakfast or that cornflakes are always to be found in the bottom left-hand shelf of the pantry. These difficulties make us realise just how unpredictable must have been the pre-placement lives of so many adopted children and also how much learning in a stable setting must take place for a child to be able to take his or her part in any social group. There is a need to study these clinical problems in more detail, to find out how common they are, to determine their natural history and, most important, to learn from parents who have coped with them. I shall turn now to various scenarios which appear to present recurring themes in practice.

Failure to improve
One major advantage of adoption is that, often for the first time, one or two adults will fight for and obtain the best educational or medical help for the child. Children thought to have learning difficulties or poor

health can, after a few years, show totally normal development. This hope – that love and stability will cure all – can be a powerful tool for change. Unfortunately the change will not always happen.

Sarah was a severely neglected child who had received almost no stimulation during her first three years of life. She had been virtually confined to a cot. When discovered she appeared like a small animal who made only grunting noises, could not walk and clung to the clothing of adults. In a short-stay foster home she improved dramatically. Then progress reached a plateau and one saw a characteristic picture of early infantile autism. The foster parents acknowledged that further progress might be very slow but still wished to adopt her. In practice they never really accepted the diagnosis of autism. and throughout Sarah's childhood they remained overwhelmed with guilt that their love had not cured her.

On a less extreme note, William was brought to the clinic by his parents. He had had an appalling first five years of life, and had then been adopted. His severe behavioural problems diminished. He developed strong loving relationships with both of the adoptive parents and his new siblings. At ten he still had minor problems with school and occasional outbursts of temper at home. His parents felt that, after five years, all problems should have disappeared. In the clinic their systematic presentation of his history and the dramatic improvements that had occurred were sufficient to reassure them that things were indeed going extremely well.

These situations are some of the very few seen in child psychiatry when simple reassurance can be of help.

Making allowances

Alice had been severely abused as a child. At ten she still had a minor physical handicap as a result. A standard punishment for her had been to lock her in the dark for many hours. Aged twelve, six years after placement, she was doing extremely well. The only problem – and one which caused very great distress – was her continual stealing of money from her parents and two brothers. This was treated with great sympathy and understanding but in family sessions it emerged how very angry her parents felt about the stealing. Had it been either of their biological sons who had done this, the result would have been a good hiding. The boys too were able to say how angry Alice made them. It was clear that Alice was sufficiently one of the family for her to be treated in exactly the same way as one of her siblings. She seemed extremely relieved when she was given an angry smack on her bottom and was sent to bed by her mother for taking a five pound note. The stealing rapidly stopped.

Clearly there is a delicate line which must be followed. Some abused children do attempt to provoke severe punishment from their parents, or can be overwhelmed by the fear of any anger being shown, but a balance can usually be found.

The adolescent identity crisis

A widely-held view is that, during adolescence, the adopted child will inevitably undergo a profound identity crisis. This notion derives from the work of Erikson who saw the identity crisis as part of normal human development. If the non-adopted adolescent has to make enormous efforts to understand who he or she is and where they come from, how much greater an effort will this be for the adopted adolescent. There is no doubt that adolescence is a time of turmoil and questioning, but empirical evidence has demonstrated that it is the rare child for whom it represents a true crisis. Most adolescents and their families do indeed survive the process, possibly a little bruised but rarely in total disarray. The same appears to be the case with adopted adolescents. They wonder about their origins and they can become disturbed, but they do appear to cope. I have yet to see a severely-disturbed adopted adolescent without other factors being present which would probably produce a similar level of disturbance in a non-adopted child. The adoption, however, acts as the peg on which the disturbance hangs.

Alix was the sixteen-year-old adopted son of professional parents. He had been placed as a baby. The family was prominent in their local community. Just after his sixteenth birthday, Alix insisted that he never wished to be seen again with his parents in the street, and that his only ambition was to find his biological mother and father. Accompanying these statements were marked changes in his behaviour. He began stealing from shops and on one occasion became involved in a vicious fight in the street, following which he was arrested. His parents insisted that theirs was a happy family; there had never been any form of problem previously. Three family interviews were fruitless, with Alix sulking and his parents complaining that they could not understand what was happening. In the fourth session there was a major explosion between the parents. They admitted that their happy marriage was a facade. They kept up the pretence both for the sake of Alix and, perhaps even more important, because of their position in the community. Alix was obviously relieved to hear this brought out into the open.

Difficulties in the adoption process

Sharon was the fourth adopted child in a family of six children. The family was obviously a happy one with a great deal of lively interaction. Only Sharon stood out as unhappy and miserable. She was persistently spiteful to the other children. The parents had wanted to adopt her when she was three months old, but legal problems had led to her having to remain in a children's home for a further year. Losing hope, the parents applied for another child. Two weeks after this child – a very demanding boy – was placed, they were contacted and told that Sharon was now free for adoption and needed to be taken urgently as the children's home she was in was about to close. She was brought to the family home by a social worker who stayed to watch her being changed and fed. The mother felt herself becoming increasingly tense and depressed and resented Sharon's arrival. After some weeks she felt that she was coping better, but very soon after that had to enter hospital for an operation during which time the father cared for the children. Fortunately, as he described it, Sharon was a quiet, passive child who needed little attention, so he could devote himself to his new son. Sharon had never really found a place in the family and rapidly developed the role of the aloof outsider. However, the resources of this family were such that Sharon was eventually helped to find a more comfortable position amongst her siblings.

Adoption is a complex process. Parents often do not anticipate the prolonged legal complications that can occur, nor the adjustments other children in the family may have to make in order to accommodate a new brother or sister. Through a series of transactions a child can become stuck in a role – becoming, for example, the permanent scapegoat of the family. Fortunately these transactions are reversable, although the longer they continue, the harder it becomes to help the family break the pattern.

Parental motivation
Professionals often ask themselves why a particular family should really want to take on a very difficult child. As the outcome for children like this is so good, it is perhaps wiser not to use concepts of unconscious motivation too readily, in attempting to decide whether a placement is indeed the right thing for a particular child and family. A 'hard-to-place' child may well satisfy the special needs of parents and, if both they and their new child benefit from this, there is no reason to complain. On occasions, however, difficulties can occur.

Mr and Mrs A had two biological children. They were a quiet, serious and deeply religious family. They adopted Anna, a vivacious, pretty seven year old, who had been physically and sexually abused. Anna's vivaciousness was somewhat excessive and she could also be aggressive, was physically overactive, and fightened her parents by her obvious sexuality. When Anna was twelve, the parents felt increasingly unable to cope, and requested treatment for her. In family interviews it became apparent that a great deal of vicarious excitement was obtained by all the family from her behaviour. Without her, they would be not so much serious as dull. The parents appeared to need an excitement which they could disapprove of. Prolonged work with them and with Anna allowed her to quieten and them to acknowledge a little more the complicated messages they were giving her. A somewhat uneasy, but far more manageable, balance was found.

Labels and genetic worries
A common reason for referral is anxiety about genetic make-up: a parental fear that a child's behaviour is a direct result of poor heredity. There is no doubt that genetic factors are of major importance in behavioural development. However, even if a child has very poor genetic loading, for example for schizophrenia, it is most unlikely that any childhood behaviour complained about would be directly due to that factor. But it is important to take these parental fears seriously and to explore both the reality of the concerns and the attitudes that lie

behind them. In most cases, factors similar to those in any other child can be found to help parents understand the origins of any problem. Some families are quite content with reassurance. They can be genuinely relieved to know that outbursts of aggression do not indicate that their son is, like his biological father was, a psychopath. Occasionally, with an older adolescent, genetic aspects are more relevant, but even here it is important to help parents move away from seeing these as a fixed unchangeable background. They can move to understanding the two-way interactions which occur between an individual's genetic make-up, and his or her environment.

Conclusion

In most cases, adoptive families and their children require the same types of evaluation and treatment as do any others who are attending child psychiatric clinics. The more experience the workers in the clinic have of adoption, the easier it becomes to recognise the common patterns that emerge and the special factors which may apply to these families. Most important, perhaps, are the lessons that current adoption practice has given to child psychiatry. It has been one of the major factors in teaching us just how resilient children are and how later care can, to a very large extent, compensate for early damage. I, and most other child psychiatrists interested in this topic, have learnt a great deal from experienced family placement social workers. There is a real need for a two-way pattern of education. Through this it should become possible to define more clearly what child psychiatrists and their colleagues are able to offer both families and agencies in post-adoption service.

References

1   Schechter M D 'Observations on adopted children' *Archives of General Psychiatry* 3, 1960.

2   Humphrey M and Ounsted C 'Adoptive families referred for psychiatric advice' *British Journal of Psychiatry* 109, 1963.

3   Pringle M L K (ed) *Adoption, facts and fallacies* Longman, 1967.

4   Wolkind S and Kozaruk A ' "Hard-to-place"? Children with medical and developmental problems' in Wedge P and Thoburn J (eds) *Finding families for 'hard-to-place' children* BAAF, 1986.

5   Lewis D O 'The treatment of adopted versus neglected delinquent children in the court' *American Journal of Psychiatry* 132, 1975.

6   Lambert L and Streather J *Children in changing families: a study of adoption and illegitimacy* Macmillan, 1980.
    Seglow J Pringle and Wedge P *Growing up adopted* NFER, 1972.

7   Wolkind S N (ed) *Medical aspects of adoption and foster care* Heinemann, 1979.

8   Bratfos O Eitinger L Tau T 'Mental illness and crime in adopted children and adoptive parents' *Acta Psychiatrica Scandinavica* 44, 1968.

THE ADOPTION AND FOSTERING WORKSHOP AT THE TAVISTOCK CLINIC
Mary Boston

There has always been a sprinkling of adoptive families seeking help at the Tavistock Clinic. Until fairly recently this mostly involved children adopted as babies. Published case studies of psychotherapy with such children (e.g. Hodges[1]) suggested that there may be certain features or issues which are particularly important for adopted children and their families. However the clinic's current focus of attention on the specific problems of adoptive families has arisen via a rather different route – from our study of severely deprived children. Several of these children had been placed for adoption after babyhood.

A considerable number of severely deprived children in care are referred to the clinic and a variety of different kinds of work has been developed in response to these referrals. There has been work with adoptive and foster families at the point of breakdown, work with new families to prevent breakdown and to help mutual adjustment and consultation for social workers and residential care staff. Some children have come into individual psychotherapy and a workshop was set up to discuss these cases, resulting in a publication.[2] A particular focus of our concern has been how we can help to facilitate mutual adjustment in a new family when the child may already be very emotionally damaged on account of his or her previous experiences. We have sometimes been doubtful whether such damaged children could settle in families, however welcoming, without specialist help for both child and family. It was our struggle with these ideas which began to bring us into contact with adoption agencies, in addition to our already well-developed links with social services departments. We noted the research indicating the advantages of adoption over foster care for later-placed children (e.g. Tizard,[3] Triseliotis[4]). We heard about Claudia Jewett's theories of 'blowing teenagers'[5] and the difficulties which could arise in adolescence in apparently well-settled placements. The need for support for adoptive parents was emphasised to us but our attention was also drawn to the dissatisfaction many adoptive parents felt about the help they received from clinics. There seemed to be situations where adopted children and their families might be urgently in need of help, yet were perhaps more reluctant than other families to seek it.

It was to address some of these issues, and to review our experience with the increasing number of children being referred who were living with families other than their birth families, that we set up our new fostering and adoption workshop. We were particularly concerned to examine the appropriateness of our responses to these families and to learn what we could about their special needs. The group meets regularly and comprises professionals of a number of disciplines: psychiatrists, psychologists, social workers and child psychotherapists, some experienced, some in training. It is a forum where current cases, in exploration or treatment, can be discussed, and where general and theoretical issues can be raised. The aim is for relevant literature to be reviewed. A research project on adoptive cases in psychotherapy is planned.

It must be said that so far the majority of children we have studied have been in foster care, so our experience in adoption is at present limited. The eight adopted children discussed have varied in age at adoption from four days to eleven years. Some families were at the initial stages of seeking help and some were in long-term treatment. All the adopted children except one had been deprived or abused before placement. Two were from an orphanage in the 'third world'. In four of the eight cases there was a difference in ethnic origin between parents and child. In all the eight families there were considerable difficulties in adjustment. Six of the children were having, or were to begin, individual psychotherapy, with the parents receiving in most cases some concurrent help. Two families were in danger of disrupting the adoption. The fourteen-year-old son of one was sent to boarding school, the sixteen-year-old daughter of the other chose to leave home, to live with her brother, after a period of therapy. In both these cases there seemed to be a temperamental and cultural mismatch between child and parents. As these are the families that have sought help from us they are obviously experiencing difficulties, but we do not know how typical they are of adoptive families as a whole.

Contrary to our expectations, adoptive and foster families shared many similar concerns. In all cases there seemed to be a vulnerable area, both for child and parents, which centred on the existence of the birth parents and the original rejection. This was true even for those adopted as babies, but of course more so when placement was later and there had been early trauma. The fantasies about birth parents, on the part of both child and new parents could be a powerful influence on the current family dynamics, colouring perceptions and making discussions and information exchange difficult. This links with research findings that adoptive and foster parents find difficulty in talking of the birth parents and that the children almost universally feel they have too little information.[6] All the children, in some form, showed signs of the search for their true identity and roots, even when apparently well settled.

The importance of *loss in adoption* needs to be recognised; there is a need to mourn the loss of the natural child in cases of infertility and the loss of the early years if an older child has joined the family. Moreover, the child always needs help in mourning the loss of the birth parents. Feelings about these losses can surface at different stages in the child's development, arousing complicated feelings in a continuing way or at times of crisis. One such crisis may be referral to the clinic, leading to a flare-up of problems. Another point of crisis in some cases has been a proposed transition from long-term fostering to adoption. This seems to arouse conflicts of loyalty and commitment in some families which had appeared to be mutually adjusted and an underlying failure of attachment may become manifest.

We have tried to address the problem of matching. How important is racial and cultural matching between children and new families? Is the current emphasis on racial matching a concrete solution to a much more complex problem? What about temperamental compatibility and how can this be evaluated? Will it grow in time, as is apparent in some cases, or are there certain mismatches which are evident at an early stage, or which could be predicted?

One question, of particular relevance for psychotherapists, is how to meet the request, which we have received more frequently lately, to help to make a child 'placeable'. Although we hope that, in time, the child may become 'easier to live with', this cannot be guaranteed and will take time and commitment from new parents as well as from the therapist. The dilemma with which we are often confronted is that if we embark upon this work, new parents are then found who are not committed to therapy or who live too far away. Therapy is then disrupted. Should we wait till the new parents are found which, for one child I am currently working with, has meant a very long wait?

A major concern in the workshop has been the appropriateness and acceptability of our attempted interventions. We have looked at about 30 cases over an academic year at different stages of work. Some have been preliminary explorations with social workers or families, some attempted assessments of children with a view to advice on placement or therapy. Others have been in the early stages of therapy or more established in therapy. We have thought about the suitability of family work. If this fails, it could feel like a second failure for those parents who have already failed to have their own children. We have often found it helpful to begin with the problems of the child. There is then sometimes more readiness for thinking in the family.

Adoptive parents feel themselves to be both more and less to blame than natural parents seeking help at a clinic (Tollemache[7]). All parents coming to the clinic tend to expect criticism but there seem in some cases, to be an additional touchiness in adoptive parents, which can present difficulties in making contact. The workers need to be resilient and aware of the ever-present threat somewhere in the minds of adoptive parents: that the child could be taken away. This may lead to a more than usually great need to prove themselves as good parents, often having unrealistic expectations of themselves and of the child. Those who try to help need to be aware that adoptive parents cannot necessarily take it for granted that the family belong together as natural parents can.

It has become clear that the assessment or selection process for adoptive parents is fraught with difficulty. Advance preparation, if not too prolonged, can sometimes be like a kind of 'pregnancy' in which the family can get adjusted to the arrival of the new member. But too often it seems the child comes very suddenly and we have found that some parents miss out on any preparation at all. The unresolved losses and conflicts then manifest themselves at the time of seeking clinic help. In one of our cases, the rejection of the parents' application for a second adopted child, when the first adoption was progressing satisfactorily, had a devastating effect on the parents and on the first adopted child. There is some evidence that the first meeting of new parents and child can be crucial, but also that attachment needs time to develop gradually. The customary probation period may be quite an impediment to this process of attachment, with a holding back of full commitment.

We have been interested in the relationships of adopted children to brothers and sisters, both natural and also adopted. We have wondered if sibling relationships are even more problematic for adopted children than for birth children, many of the parents' complaints focussing on such rivalries and jealousies. The adopted child's integration among other brothers and sisters may require more consideration.

The more extreme children's problems reported in the literature, such as arson, violence, delinquency and running away, applied in our limited experience in the workshop more to the fostered than the adopted children. This seemed a significant and interesting observation but would need to be supported by further cases. One adopted child was suspected of violence and delinquency and another of sexual activity (both adolescents) but the other children seemed much more split between the struggle to be the good child and eruptions of bad behaviour, sometimes involving cruelty. Often there were psychosomatic symptoms. The child's fantasies about the birth parents and the reasons for the adoption exert a powerful influence on their current behaviour. One little girl put her conflict very poignantly: 'My first mother did not know how to look after me, she left me in a donjon . . . no, my first mother was not naughty, it's a lie, I was bad.'

References

1   Hodges J 'Two crucial questions. Adopted children in psychoanalytic treatment' *Journal of Child Psychotherapy* 10, 1984.

2   Boston M and Szur R (eds) *Psychotherapy with severely-deprived children* Routledge and Kegan Paul, 1983.

3   Tizard B *Adoption, a second chance* Open Books, 1977.

4   Triseliotis J (ed) *New developments in foster care and adoption* Routledge and Kegan Paul, 1980.

5   Unpublished: see reference in Chapter 6.

6   See 4 above.

7   Tollemache L 'Choices and losses/losses and choices in adoption' Tavistock
    Clinic paper (unpublished) 1985.

FAMILY THERAPY: WORK WITH FAMILIES IN LATE ADOPTION
John Byng-Hall, Gill Gorell Barnes, Caroline Lindsey and Christine Heath

A group of family therapists at the Tavistock Clinic have been meeting
in order to devise ways of working with families with late adopted and
fostered children who present serious problems. Often the child is at
risk of being removed from the home. The therapist sees all members
of the family together. Because every relationship affects every other
relationship in the family, this makes it possible to use all the family
resources to influence the attachment between the adopted child and
his or her family. The way in which these attachment patterns have
evolved is of crucial importance.

In birth or early adoption families, the 'scripts' for family relationships
have evolved over time: they are shared. Late adoptions involve a
process of matching the new entrant's script with that of the adoptive
family. This process has to take into account the discrepancies between
the two scripts. The adoptive family has, by definition, a space in its
script for another member. This space is never a complete vacuum:
there are expectations and fantasies – partly based on the past – about
how the role will be filled and what the child will mean to them. There is
great variety in the degree to which this role is precisely scripted – say,
to fit into a dead member's image – as opposed to providing the
freedom for the child to create a new role for her or himself. This is true
for all families but the gap which is left unfilled by a birth child has its
own particular disappointments and hopes. The adoptive child's own
script for relationships is also likely to be highly complex and will of
course include the prediction that he or she will be rejected by one set of
parents and taken on by someone else. The child will probably arrive
with two main strategies for dealing with this, a superficially charming
script to gain acceptance, and an escalating rejecting script which pre-
empts the anticipated rejection by the adoptive family.

The quality of the bonding depends on the fit between the two
scripts. This fit depends partly on 'falling in love' because each – at least
partially – can be the other's dream; but it also depends on how

discrepancies between the hopes and the actual experience are managed. As the child brings segments of his or her disruptive script into the family, each is potentially confronted by the fact that the gap is not to be filled as promised in the honeymoon phase. If upsetting behaviour within the family is discovered not to lead to the feared catastrophe of break-up, the difficult experiences can be integrated into a new shared family script. If disruption looms, then the most dangerous elements in the interaction may be avoided only to erupt later – often in adolescence – because the original incompatable aspects of each script have remained unaltered. If the two scripts are kept apart – perhaps one acted out at school – they cannot influence each other.

All this is familiar enough. What are the implications? A family approach allows all the experiences in therapy to be added to the shared evolving script. For example, drawing family trees of both family and child can be a powerful way of strengthening bonds, including those to new siblings. Life stories or books done separately miss this opportunity. Work can also be done to help modify difficult interaction which is then less feared and can be experienced as shared rather than belonging exclusively to the child.

Many ways of working utilise the energy of bonding to create change. Clearly the way that children come into the family alters the form that this energy takes. Birth is largely a 'gut level' instinctive joining: adoption and fostering involve a reflective reviewing process. Indeed, many of the processes of adoption necessitate a damping-down of gut level responses because of the scrutiny by others, prior to and during the bonding process, based on the requirements to conform to outsiders' ideas of 'adequate' parenting. This has its hazards as well as its strengths. Both giving birth and adopting, of course, involve thinking and feeling, nevertheless setting the seal on membership is via a very different route. It does not imply that one is superior to the other; it does, however, mean that the way to break the seal is seen as being different. This is very important. Reviewing the relationship with outsiders is more likely to be experienced as a setting for untying the bond because that was how it all started in the first place.

One fourteen-year-old boy had been adopted at eight after many changes of foster parents and house parents. In the first ten minutes of the first family session when asked what he wanted to see changed in the family he said that he wanted to change his parents. Quite appropriately, in family therapy terms, the therapist explored with him how, now that he was adopted, he could not change his parents, although he had previously changed his foster parents. In a birth family, to get to the underlying tension – and this was certainly it – so soon would be good practice. The therapist would be picking up one side of intense ambivalence, and could rely on the energy of the underlying attachment to emerge. The alternative of changing aspects of the relationship, but not the people, could then be discussed. In this family, however, it started a process of reviewing that ended in the boy leaving home.

Therapists who assume that their contract to help change what goes on between people is understood, must remember that, in these families, merely meeting with outside authorities is likely to give rise to the assumption that the 'real' agenda is separation. Any discussion of fantasies or fears of breakdown must be seen within this context. In general, we have found that symptoms of all degrees of severity within late adoption or fostering can herald a very rapidly escalating breakdown in the placement, and that family therapy may not be as effective in reversing the process as would be expected from work that we have done with birth families in which rejection is impending. Indeed, in retrospect, we are often left feeling that our role has been to preside over an untying process which was inevitable and perhaps necessary from the beginning. We can be helpful in this.

In contrast, another interesting observation has been that in some long-term fosterings, impending adoption precipitates a breakdown, rather than cementing the relationship as expected. This would suggest that the additional distance provided by fostering can, in some instances, be crucial.

Family work also reveals the problems of families in which some of the children are being adopted and others are not. In one family the most insecurely placed of the children was being adopted in order to secure his long-term future. A girl who had been with the family the longest was not. Rational discussion of the reason for this appeared to be understood but the incomprehensibility of bureaucracy could not be denied, especially when yet another child (the sixth) was placed with the family because it was such a good family. Because local authorities often do not see the whole family together they may not see just how disturbing such events can be to the other attachments. This girl's placement broke down.

As yet, it is not clear how much our relative failure in maintaining the bonds is because techniques effective with birth families need further modification in foster and adoptive families, or because the nature of the attachments in late adoption and fostering of damaged children are more prone to break down. In those cases in which we have been successful, the intensity of the child's bonding to his or her adoptive family seems to be the important variable, rather than the degree of severity of problems.

The whole experience has left us fascinated, puzzled and quite humble. A family approach, however, has great potential.

SUPPORT FOR FAMILIES WITH ADOPTED ADOLESCENTS

Claudia Jewett is a family psychotherapist from Boston, Massachusets, whose work with adopters and their adolescent children is becoming increasingly influential both in the USA and in Britain. In October 1986 she came to the UK to speak at a series of conferences organised by the National Foster Care Association. She also led two workshops set up by the Parents for Children adoption agency: the first for members of the adoption panel and parents with adopted adolescents, the second for 35 workers from a variety of disciplines with a special interest in and experience of teenage adoptions. The following is a summary of some of Claudia Jewett's comments and ideas, reported by Hedi Argent.

Does adoption work? Critics of adoption are inclined to quote the large number of adopted children both in care and in trouble who are receiving treatment. Statistics can be made to sound alarming. In fact, the evidence in the USA is that only thirteen out of every hundred children in treatment are adopted. This figure is barely higher than the percentage of adopted people in the community.

Claudia Jewett has based her observations on a study of 80 families with adopted adolescents who have left home precipitously, explosively and at a younger age than would normally be expected. Not knowing how to separate, rather than not being attached, is identified as the problem and we are urged to look carefully at how to prepare parents and children to become a family – and that includes ultimately leaving home. Do we, in fact, prepare them for separation, or do we leave them feeling that to bond with each other and to attach to one another is all? We should be asking potential adopters to examine their own separation experiences. How did they themselves leave home? Did they fulfil their own parents' expectations in the way they became independent? How do they think children become adult? How do they imagine their adopted child will leave them? And what are the separation patterns in the adopted child's birth family? Too often their birth mother will have left home too young because she was pregnant or in some kind of conflict with school or the law.

If we accept that infants learn to separate from their mother-figures between 18 and 36 months, then we must also accept that how they learn to do so during this period is critical. How does the infant safely climb down from the mother's lap to explore the great world? If the mother is too anxious about the dark and danger, she will make separation unsafe. If she pushes the child off her lap and outside without a care, then she will make separation harsh and rejecting, and if she is not there when the child comes back she will lay the foundation for the deepest insecurity about leaving anything or anybody. Only if the mother can help her child explore without fear, but carefully; if she can be ready with a plaster for minor cuts, and always be where she said she would be, can the child learn that it is alright to go when you are ready and come back when you have had enough. And that the process need not hurt the leaver or the left. Very few adopted adolescents have been lucky enough to learn this. They are much more likely to play out their negative reaction to separation by either clinging to their new family in a distressed or distressing way, or by exploding out of the family because that is easier than an orderly separation when you do not know how to separate at all.

The questions for adopters are: can they create an environment which can be safely left and returned to? Can they wait and watch their adopted child experiment with separation patterns rooted deep in their infancy? Children may have to take the risk they have been rescued from. One legend of adoption is, 'We adopted you to make you safe and happy', but adolescents, on the whole, do not feel safe or happy. Adopted children may have to check out: 'How would I have got on somewhere else?'.

One girl of eighteen could not allow herself to remain with her adoptive family until she had cut loose and lived as a prostitute, like her own young mother had done. Only then could she finally find out that her mother's way need not become her way, that she did not have to act out a curse and that she could now choose her adoptive family as they had once chosen her.

A boy of seventeen had to live rough and experiment with drugs in the downtrodden neighbourhood where he was born, before he could fulfil his own and his adoptive parents' wishes: to go to university and get an honours degree.

Adolescence is always a time of renegotiation. Adopted children and their parents need to renegotiate the roles they have assigned to each other.

All parents create roles for all their children, but these are more likely to emerge gradually and appropriately for home-grown children, who do not bring the unknown trailing behind them. Even so, we know that conflicts can ensue when children fall short of their parents' expectations during adolescence. Children placed in substitute families may have to fulfil ready-made roles in order to fit into the family in the first place. As adolescents they may have to reject these roles and renegotiate different ones acceptable to themselves and to their adoptive families. This may happen even when a child has been placed for adoption many years before adolescence. When the assigned role shatters it is shattering for the parents. The more they try to hold on to the shattered shards the more hurt they will be, the more rigid they will become. They will have to renegotiate their own parental roles in order to survive. No one can remain the dependable mopping-up mother for ever. Half an hour at a time is all the devastated parents of a disruptive daughter who is staying out at night may be able to manage, when the daughter decides to come home at all. Letting go some broken pieces releases the tension but does not change love and affection. 'Letting go with love' is a useful slogan for all parents of adolescents and an essential one for adopters.

While adoptive parents and explosive teenagers still manage to live together, certain home improvements can make life more tolerable. When set meals are a problem, a buffet will avoid the endless discussion about the menu and table manners. Parents can only offer what they have, make the choice attractive and occasionally change the dishes. They cannot force their growing child to feed. Adopters may know what they ought to do, they may know what they want to do but they must acknowledge what they can do and do it, and do no more. Yet there is hope. In Claudia Jewett's study the adopted adolescents are growing into adopted young people in their twenties and even those who left precipitously when they were in their late teens are coming back to their adoptive families if the door has been left open.

Claudia Jewett has a final word for the worker. Do not work with adoptive families and adolescents if you think adoption is not as good as home-grown. Parents and children who need help to separate do not need help to end the adoption. You either believe in adoption or you do not.

7 After adoption in America

Hedi Argent

In 1985 I was fortunate enough to be awarded a Churchill Travel Fellowship and to be given leave by my agency, Parents for Children, to study post-adoption services in the USA at first hand. Although I travelled and studied for six weeks I could, in that time, cover only a fraction of that country and see only examples of what is being offered after adoption. I tried to see as many workers and consumers as possible and I corresponded with many I could not meet. Everywhere I went, I was impressed by the enthusiasm and energy of the people involved in adoption. We still have much to learn from our transatlantic colleagues, especially about working in groups and about using therapy. But it was rewarding to hear from them that they are watching our progress too and learning from our experience, especially in post-adoption work. It was also reassuring to know that we are all struggling with the same problems. As Betsy Cole from the North American Welfare League put it, 'We have to settle the first question first: Is post-adoption service a drip we set up to meet a crisis or is it an immunisation to prevent the crisis?'.

In America, everything is big, and adoption is no exception. In the United Kingdom we may work diligently in our individual corners to find families for children with special needs but in America our colleagues work in the middle of the ring under the blazing lights of the ministries, the media and the masses. Money, methods and motivation are continually scrutinised and have to be justified. Results are used as evidence. New ideas and developments have to be cost-effective. A post-adoption service may not be a best buy.

The USA has led the way in adoption of children with special needs. We have modelled our agencies on them and we have been inspired by their confidence and inventiveness. But in spite of their ten-year lead, they are barely ahead in setting up services for families who have adopted although they are way ahead in putting it down on paper. The 'Model statement on post-legal adoption services' was published by a 'specially convened North America post-legal adoption committee' in

June 1984, as a guideline to the individual states which are responsible for adoption law. It deals with the purposes and rationale, methods and resources, administrative structures and financial basis for post-adoption services. (What a pity that we do not, or will not, use words as effectively.) The aim of the model statement is to provide a comprehensive and unlimited service for all the parties to adoption. This does not differ from some British plans but it is worth noting the differences inherent in practice and culture which must finally influence the shape of any service.

Americans are not inhibited, it seems, about money. They expect to be adequately paid for what they do and they do not mind talking about it. On the other hand they expect to give, as well as to get, good value for their money. Adoption subsidy, which we would call an approved adoption allowance, paid according to federal law, is generous and flexible. It is not means-tested and is attached to a child's special needs. It can be geared to meet medical, educational or emotional needs in the future. For instance, in Michigan a subsidy was increased to pay for daily analysis for a girl of fourteen who was adopted as a disturbed ten year old. The availability of cash to cover a crisis goes a long way towards providing the backbone for a post-adoption service in America. In the UK the approved adoption allowance is too patchy, too rigid and, apart from a few exceptions, too reluctantly given to be considered as part of an overall service to adoptive families.

If present trends continue in both countries there will be a basic difference not in the aims but in the delivery of post-adoption services. In the UK we are looking to *adoption agencies* to fund and provide a support service after adoption. The Post-Adoption Centre in London is, so far, the only exception. In America, on the whole, adoption agencies are trying to find the funding to pay for outside services and they are encouraging existing community services to meet more of the needs. In 1985 the federal government financed agencies to run four experimental post-adoption schemes. Each agency is responding to requests for help by using outside specialists to provide that help. Not one of these – or any of the other schemes I came across – provide a formalised post-adoption service as of right for all adoptive families. Some agencies hold an annual social event, some agencies offer advice and counselling when approached, some lead support groups. The Children's Home Society of Minnesota probably offers one of the most comprehensive and established services for adopters, adopted people and birth families which includes training, counselling and group work. But even this service, freely available, does not take the initiative and it is unclear how many of the agency's hundreds of baby adopters, adopted people and relinquishing parents are, or have been, involved. Other agencies too numerous to mention are developing similar programmes. Of the statutory state agencies the Department of Adoptions in the county of Los Angeles leads the way with a streamlined range of services which cater for every possible need arising out of adoption. Again, however, it is a service that invites and responds but does not instigate a follow-up. On the whole, American agencies are more concerned with the rights of adopted adults than we need be, because these rights vary from state to state and are not always well-defined. But we have much to learn from the American adoption agencies' concern for birth parents.

Therapy is accepted as normal and necessary in America and has to be paid for. Spaulding for Children in Michigan, which has pioneered adoption of children with special needs, is training its own workers to become therapists in order to attract funds for post-adoption work from the state adoption subsidy. This service, to be called the Family Preservation Project, will not be seen as a continuation of post-placement support but as a response to adoptive families in times of crisis. The therapists will not be part of the placement team but will be available for training and advice to other therapists throughout the State of Michigan, in adoption work. America already has a Centre for Adoptive Families. This is a private family therapy centre in New York City which takes referrals directly from adoptive families. It promotes active change and challenges the 'maintenance support' approach advocated by the mutual support groups. Other therapies and therapists and psychotherapy centres have entered the adoption field. Some private therapists specialise in adoption and some clinics and child care departments are collaborating to develop techniques to help adoptive families, notably Anne Hartmann at Ann Arbor University in Michigan, Joyce Forsythe who is working on 'holding' and dietary therapies, Vera Fahlberg who regards preparation and post-adoption support as one process, and Claudia Jewett who has been doing revelatory work with explosive adopted adolescents and their families (see Chapter 6).

Although there is no health service, a free counselling service is provided by most education authorities, and adoption agencies are increasingly requesting help in schools for their adoptive families. Children with disabilities are fully integrated into the ordinary school system in most states, and there is a great deal of parent participation. Some adopters feel more confident using educational services than having to admit to the adoption agency that they have a problem. Over here, schools must refer to child guidance clinics, which can immediately make families feel self-conscious and different.

Encouraged by their adoption agencies, Americans, who seem to form groups so much more easily than their British counterparts, are setting up mutual support groups in numerous shapes and sizes to involve adopters, adopted people and birth parents. There are, in America, some national adoptive parent organisations like COHAC (Counsel on Adoptable Children) and OURS (Organisation for a United Response) which are similar to our own PPIAS and which also offer advice and guidance, but there are also the more informal groups which seem to spring up spontaneously whenever there are enough people who share the same interests. There are groups for single parents, for inter-country adopters, for single fathers, for parents of adolescents, for birth parents, for baby adopters, for ethnic minorities and for families which have disrupted. Some of them are started off or administered by social workers, but most of them are not. They raise funds, advocate for each other, recruit more families, organise themselves to be heard and have an influence on adoption policy. I observed in America a zest for groups, in contrast to the reluctance to join I frequently encounter in my work with adopters here, and a greater trust in mutual support rather than professional services.

One major difference between the two countries will affect a post-adoption service for both. There is a new word in American adoption: it is 'dissolution'. It appears that in several states adoption, like marriage, can be dissolved. The adoptive parents can go to court and apply to dissolve the adoption if they can prove that it has irretrievably broken down. Our own experience with adopted adolescents makes it painfully clear that irretrievable breakdown feels like an ever-present possibility when older children have been placed with families. But we take it for granted that the families we work with regard even their estranged adopted children as still their children. Some American adoption workers were amazed to hear that British families were prepared to hang on in almost any circumstances. Kay Donley from New York Spaulding for Children, explained: 'We're a throw-away society – if something doesn't work, we fix it. If we can't fix it, we get rid of it.

Dissolution is still rare even in the USA although it is much talked about. And there is always the danger – greater in America because everything is greater – that, like disruption, it will fast become a fashionable word and then a fashion. In any case, an American post-adoption service will certainly have to take into account the possibility of a legal ending.

In October 1985 a national conference on post-legal adoption services was held in Minneapolis. Two hundred delegates were planned for, over 400 registered in advance and nearly 500 turned up, reflecting the high degree of current interest in the subject. It is more than an interest. It is a concerned response to an increasingly perceived need – a need evident in inter-country adoption, transracial adoption and traditional baby adoptions. David Kirk, who was the main speaker at the conference, drew attention to the diverging needs of child and parents in baby adoptions, which can cause conflict if unheeded. For as the child grows and needs to know more about roots and history, so the parents' need to know recedes, because their adopted child has become their own.

Warnings were signalled at the conference about 'open adoption', another fashionable phrase which could lead to fashionable practice. Two groups of adopted children with continuing contact with birth parents have been found to be more disturbed than groups of adopted children without contact – but the lack of adequate preparation and support, rather than the contact itself, was said to be the cause of the children's distress. Jo Prouty of the Children's Home Society in Minnesota considered adopted children's groups to be a necessary 're-cycling' process. As children develop, their perceptions change and their understanding of adoption and their place in the family needs regular re-examination outside the family. She meets with the same children for a series of sessions every two years. This is the kind of post-adoption work which needs to be built in at the time of placement. No agency in the UK is offering anything of the kind so far and it was the only example I encountered in America of professional immunisation rather than the saline drip in a crisis.

It is now three years since the model statement was published, two years since the international conference in Minneapolis. New ventures in post-adoption services are happening all the time across the Atlantic, as they are here. Project Impact, which heads a network of agencies in

Boston, Massachusetts, last year set up an 'intensive crisis-orientated intervention service for legalised families'. There is now a 'National Resource Centre for Special Needs Adoption' in Chelsea, Michigan. In October 1986 there was a second conference on post-adoption service in Boston. Twelve workshops were led by practitioners who are involved in new ventures. They are leading the field but we are watching them. It is good to know that they are also watching us.

8 The way ahead

Hedi Argent

Sections 1 and 2 of the 1975 Children Act place a duty on every local authority in England and Wales to provide a comprehensive adoption service to adopted people, adoptive families and birth parents. It has taken more than twelve years for this part of the Act to come into force. In Scotland, similar arrangements already exist.

A post-adoption service is not mentioned in the Act but a service could not be comprehensive if it were to cease at the point of legal adoption. Soon therefore it should not be a question of whether post-adoption support is available but rather how it is offered and by whom it is delivered.

It is already evident, from the post-adoption work described here, that there is a whole range of needs and that a variety of responses is possible. What is on offer will perhaps determine who becomes the consumer. Thus, the Triangle Group in Nottingham, while attracting birth parents and adopted people, is not attracting many adopters, whereas many users of the Post-Adoption Centre in London are adoptive parents. It is unlikely that any one agency will be able to provide a truly comprehensive service but there is room, under the Act, for co-operation and partnership between statutory, voluntary and specialist organisations. It is to be hoped that imaginative and mutually rewarding arrangements will be made and that vigorous post-adoption services will be one of the results.

We are only just beginning to learn, from the families who adopt, the children who are adopted, and the parents who relinquish their children for adoption, what it is they require from us. It is therefore essential to share and exchange our experiences with each other. A network of agencies operating some kind of post-adoption service was formed a year ago and meets regularly.

We support and encourage each other and monitor each other's plans and schemes. There will be a place and a need for other such network groups as more agencies, either separately or together, take on responsibility for post-adoption work.

Although subsidised adoptions are the backbone of American post-adoption support, hardly a mention has been made by the contributors to this book of approved adoption allowances. Adoption allowances in this country are eccentrically varied. They reflect differing attitudes to adoption rather than special needs of children. Thus, one borough will readily pay whatever is necessary to enable children to be adopted who might otherwise have remained in care, while another local authority will reaveal its distaste for adopters who need financial help by awarding a niggardly sum which simply does not help enough. A third authority may not have a scheme to pay any allowance at all. There is a suspicion about people who do something worthy but want to be paid for it, but there is certainly nothing worthy about being chronically short of money. It is not likely to make adopters better parents. And I have yet to meet anyone who will go to the lengths of adoption in order to increase their income! Our post-adoption services will not become comprehensive until we have sorted out this question of money.

The next issue we will have to come to grips with is access by birth families after adoption. Access has as many meanings as the approved adoption allowance has levels. Access can mean anything from an occasional supervised meeting on neutral ground, with a grandmother, to regular direct contact between adopted child and birth parents. Contact can mean birthday and Christmas cards or it can mean unlimited telephone calls and letters. 'Open adoption' is a fairly new phrase. We have to make sure it does not become merely a new fashion. We have to remind ourselves always that we must serve the best interests of the child. Adoption has moved a long way from providing a service for childless couples to providing the best available families for children. Perhaps access after adoption is our next door. Let us open it gently.

Useful addresses

Lothian Adopters' Group (LAG)
27 Belmont Road, Edinburgh EH14 5OZ.

The National Organisation for the Counselling of Adoptees and Parents (NORCAP)
3 New High Street, Headington, Oxford OX3 7AJ.

The Meeting Place
A new, free access facility in Central London from The Thomas Coram Foundation for Children. Organiser, Stephen Gaston, 01-278 2424.

Parent-to-Parent Information on Adoption Services (PPIAS)
Lower Boddington, Daventry, Northamptonshire NN11 6YB.

The Post-Adoption Centre
Interchange Building, 15 Wilkin Street, London NW5 3NG.

The Tavistock Clinic
120 Belsize Lane, London NW3.

The Triangle Group
8 Kingston Road, West Bridgford, Nottingham NG2 7AQ.

British Agencies for Adoption & Fostering

British Agencies for Adoption and Fostering (BAAF) is a registered charity and professional association for all those working in the child care field. BAAF's work includes:

providing training and consultation services to social workers and other professionals to help them improve the quality of medical, legal and social work services to children and families;

giving evidence to government committees on subjects concerning children and families;

responding to consultative documents on changes in legislation and regulations affecting children in or at risk of coming into care;

publishing a wide range of books, training packs and leaflets as well as a quarterly journal on adoption, fostering and child care issues;

giving advice and information to members of the public on aspects of adoption, fostering and child care issues;

and helping to find new families for children through the BAAF Exchange Service, 'Be My Parent' and 'Find a Family'.

More information about BAAF (including membership subscription details) can be obtained from BAAF, 11 Southwark Street, London SE1 1RQ.